Edward Paget-Tomlinson's

A ⇌ Z of the

Birmingham Canal Navigations

Historical notes by Ray Shill

BCNS

A BCNS book

A‑Z of the Birmingham Canal Navigations

Edward Paget-Tomlinson
and **Ray Shill**

Edited by Martin O'Keeffe and Peter Silvester

Published May 2016 for Birmingham Canal Navigations Society
by Canal Book Shop
Audlem Mill Limited The Wharf Audlem Cheshire CW3 0DX

ISBN 978-0-9574037-8-9

CONTENTS

The Birmingham Canal Navigations Society (BCNS) aims to conserve, improve and encourage a wide range of interests in the 100 mile network of the Birmingham and Black Country Waterways known as the BCN.

It was formed in 1968, and has been promoting the area's canal system since then. In the early days, it fought campaigns against the closure of many canals, but now the emphasis is on restoration and promoting awareness.

The BCNS has its headquarters at the restored Pumphouse on the Titford Canal, in Oldbury. At 511 ft above sea level, the Pumphouse is at the highest part of the BCN. Around the pumphouse are moorings, both for visitors and long term.

We meet monthly at the Pumphouse for talks by a wide variety of speakers on canals and subjects of related interest. See www.bcnsociety.co.uk for details. A fair proportion of members are boaters, so we do not have meetings across the summer, as many are out boating. We also run boating events and rallies around the BCN.

Members are kept up to date with news and events around the region by the quarterly magazine 'Boundary Post' (named after the posts that once lined the edges of the BCN marking the canal company boundary).

The Society works closely with the Canal & River Trust to ensure the ongoing maintenance of the local system. The BCNS has CRT recognised self-supervising work party status. We hold regular work parties throughout the year using the society's purpose built 38ft workboat *Phoenix*, paired with open butty *Crow*.

Why not join us, and help us conserve this valuable labyrinth of canals and its heritage for the benefit of everyone? Please contact the BCN Society via www.bcnsociety.com

The BCNS was established as a Registered Charity (charity number: 1091760) in 1968. In 2002, it was reconstituted as a Company Limited by Guarantee (company number: 4306537).

FOREWORD

In early 1997, I was Editor of the Birmingham Canal Navigations Society journal 'Boundary Post'. Named after the BCN's iconic cast iron territorial markers, the magazine had been in existence from the very early days of the Society, founded in 1968 in response to the many threats to the Birmingham canals perceived at the time.

BCNS Chairman Martin O'Keeffe told me he'd been in contact with Edward Paget-Tomlinson, maritime and waterways historian, artist, museum curator and one time owner of the Thomas Clayton boat *Gifford*. Edward had agreed to produce a series of pen and ink drawings of scenes based on our local waterways under the heading of 'An A-Z of the BCN'. Imagine my editorial delight when I realised these were to form the centrepiece of 'Boundary Post' for the next 26 quarterly issues, over six years' worth of material! Imagine my even greater joy when Martin went on to say that each drawing was to be accompanied by an article by local transport historian and author of many waterways related books, Ray Shill.

And so the series progressed – from *A is for Anglesey Basin* to *Z is for Zinc* - encompassing a whole spectrum of Birmingham and Black Country boats, industries and locations. Each subject illustrated with one of Edward's meticulously drawn studies, illuminated and elucidated by Ray's articles based on his deep knowledge of the system founded on years of research.

Over a decade has passed since the series ended. Old 'Boundary Posts' have been consigned to the skips of history and we feel that it's high time that such an important contribution to our knowledge about the BCN should receive a wider airing.

Phil Clayton

INTRODUCTION

The production of these drawings and articles is the result of some happy coincidences. The first of these was that my employer British Rail was in the early part of the 1990s undergoing a complete re-organisation prior to rail privatisation, which resulted in my job being transferred to Birmingham.

This move was to Regional Railways Central, based in offices located in Stanier House in Holliday Street. Of course this was just around the corner from Gas Street basin, and I looked out over the old Central TV studios and what was then the Holiday Inn. Both of these were, as I was to discover, on what had been the terminal basin of the Birmingham Canal Navigations at Paradise Wharf.

We had on occasions to go to one of the other railway offices in Birmingham, at Quayside Tower in Broad Street, so then had to walk there via Gas Street basin. This intrigued me to find out more about the canal network, and through another coincidence I soon realised that amongst the other Regional Railways Central employees was Ray Shill who was in charge of the stores at Birmingham New Street station. I took the opportunity to introduce myself to Ray, and having similar interests together, we explored the BCN further afield than central Birmingham. In reality, Ray knew so much about this but was happy to share his knowledge and show me around.

In order to find out more about the BCN, I searched out the BCN Society and joined up and got involved with things, firstly becoming sales officer and later as chairman. My association with the Society continues to this day.

In issue 8 of 'Archive' magazine (published by Black Dwarf Lightmoor in Lydney, Glos.), the artist and historian Edward Paget-Tomlinson started a series titled *The A to Z of Sailing Craft*. These consisted of a drawing of a boat together with a description. Of course Edward had produced a long running series in 'Waterways World', *The Colours of the Cut*, of colour profiles of narrowboats and barges.

At that time, Neil Parkhouse the publisher of 'Archive', operated a bookshop in Lydney and on a visit I noticed some of Edward's watercolours on display. I enquired if Edward would undertake commissions and Neil indicated he would and gave me the contact details.

I have never been one for 'cold calling' and when I rang Edward it was with some trepidation, indeed this was not helped by a slightly terse response. However I was invited down to Edward's home in Somerset to discuss a commission. I set off with some nervousness, but this was dispelled on meeting Edward as we of course had very similar interests, and a happy day was spent discussing canals and railways. Edward also had a large archive of pictures including lots of BCN ones, so I eagerly looked through those! I also realised that Edward had the same dislike for the phone that I had, thus explaining his initial reaction!

Following on from a commission for a painting of a BCN scene, it occurred to me that a series similar to that in 'Archive' would make an attractive one for the BCN Society magazine 'Boundary Post'. Thus was born the idea for the BCN A-Z. Thankfully, Edward was happy to prepare the drawings and Ray Shill the text. Ray and I discussed the subjects and came up with ideas for the scenes; this of course required some head scratching for some letters of the alphabet such as Q, X and Z. However within the twenty six illustrations, I think we have covered many aspects of the BCN!

The 'A-Z of the Birmingham Canal Navigations' is therefore a tribute both to Edward Paget-Tomlinson, a skilled and knowledgeable artist who prepared these drawings with much enthusiasm, and to Ray Shill who has done so very much to record the history of not only the BCN but many other waterways and railways. Ray continues to write articles for 'Boundary Post', but Edward sadly died in 2003, having left us a lasting legacy in his art and also the many books that he wrote.

Martin O'Keeffe
President, BCNS
February 2016

ACKNOWLEDGEMENTS

The Editors thank Richard Dean (Canalmaps Archive - www.canalmaps.net) for his detailed map of the BCN system.

Photo credits are given where known. Many photos are certainly out of copyright. The publisher has attempted to identify copyright owners, and credit will be given in future editions if copyright owners contact the publisher.

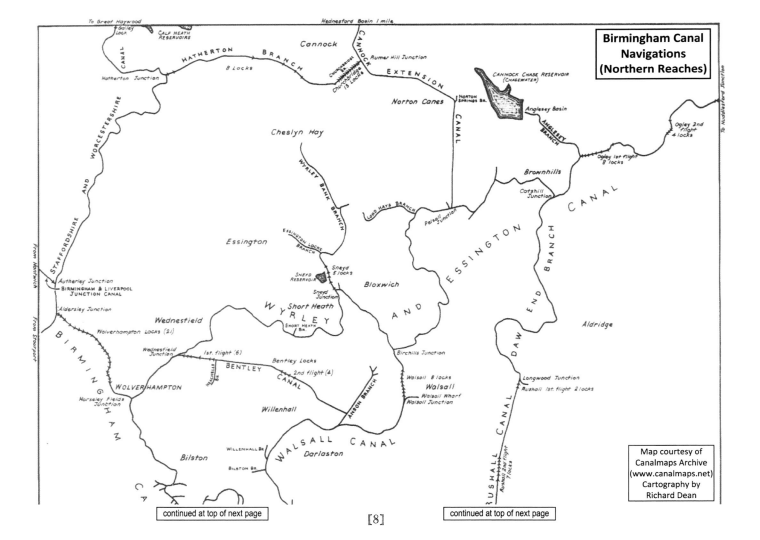

Birmingham Canal
Navigations
(Northern Reaches)

continued at top of next page

continued at top of next page

[[8]]

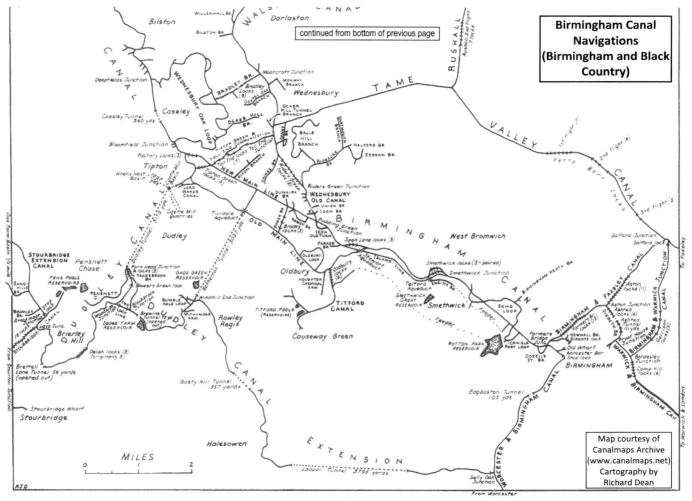

continued from bottom of previous page

A is for Anglesey Basin

Deep coal mining ceased in Britain during December 2015; this was the end of an era. Wherever coal existed, it has been taken by open work or by making headings underground. In South Staffordshire and East Worcestershire, now most commonly known as the Black Country, the coal was often mined digging shafts to the various coal seams to extract the coal.

Demand for coal increased from the end of the eighteenth century as the local iron smelting and working industry prospered. That demand was bolstered by a host of other industries that came to the district, such as brick making, glass making and the working of non-ferrous metals such as brass, which became a staple trade in Birmingham. Then there was also the increasing domestic demand for coal as the population increased through new jobs in industry or the various service trades. The canals brought boat-load upon boat-load of coal to the wharves and factories placed along the canal side of the Birmingham Canal Navigations.

As the various seams of coal became exhausted, new sources were looked for. The search for coal led to the deeper measures, which required more extensive plant to extract it. A particularly large resource of untapped coal lay under the area known as Cannock Chase. Whilst this happened at the dawn of railway network, canals were also extended to this region in order to bring coal to the established industries in Birmingham and the Black Country.

James Walker, engineer, was responsible for the major upgrading of the BCN. Through his skills and the skills of his associates, the Tame Valley Canal (opened 1844) was made.

Since the demise of the Cannock coalfield, Angelsey Basin now displays a much more rural and tranquil vista; looking down from the reservoir dam.

Walker planned the Cannock Extension that eventually was finished to Hednesford Basin (in 1863), which brought coal on to the canal from the collieries at Norton Canes, Cannock and Hednesford.

The first major water link to the deep mines on Cannock Chase was the widening of the existing feeder to the former Wyrley & Essington Canal Reservoir, Chasewater, near Norton Canes. The Wyrley had merged with the BCN during 1839. Following this merger, the Wyrley and Essington was upgraded, and three new links constructed that joined the two systems. These new links acted as an encouragement for the improvement of trade throughout the BCN network and at the heart of that trade was the movement of coal. The Anglesey Branch was well placed to serve a variety of markets.

At first, the reservoir feeder carried that water to a point near Ogley Top Lock and included a short tunnel section. This feeder was widened out into a proper canal between 1850 and 1851 to accommodate the mining operations of the Marquis of Anglesey. Essentially, the new canal followed the route of the original feeder, but there was a point north of the A5 where it deviated slightly.

Anglesey Basin became the terminus of the BCN Anglesey Branch Canal. This canal was made so that the canal might serve the Hammerwich Colliery, whose shafts lay at the foot of the Eastern Dam for Cannock Chase Reservoir.

Cannock Chase Reservoir has been known by several names; Norton and Cannock Wood are two which appear in archive texts. Cannock Chase was the name by which BCN records and maps usually refer, but today it is called Chasewater. Since its construction in 1800, the reservoir has provided water for the canal system.

The canal opened out into a wide basin below the dam to enable boats to be stored or turned if necessary. For day boats, which could be steered from either end, the space was used to keep the empty boats prior to loading.

Hammerwich Colliery began raising coal in 1849, and was followed in 1852 by the Uxbridge Colliery. When Uxbridge was finished, a standard gauge railway was completed to the South Staffordshire Railway, and coal was shipped out by waggon.

This railway ran beside the Anglesey Branch, and a loading wharf was constructed to transfer coal from railway waggons to canal boats. Pit tubs straight out of the mine were loaded into the waggons and conveyed along the railway to the wharf. Here they were taken out, wheeled across the wharf and the contents tipped into the waiting vessels.

Mining operations were expanded by the Cannock Chase Colliery Company who took over the mines in 1854. Eventually, ten pits came into production, linked by a common railway system. Anglesey Basin became one of several shipping points for the coal, but the traffic was usually heavy and the canal was often crowded with loaded and empty boats.

Loading Coal at Anglesey Basin. Sight Seen Partnership filmed a recreated coal run in September 1999 for a video 'Last Coal Run from Anglesey'. The tug is *Enterprise,* previously owned by Ernest Thomas, and later, Bernard Hales and Partners.
Brenda Ward

Before the main collieries closed, gatherings of boats here were quite common. Open iron and wooden day boats would clog the waterway so that it was possible to pass from bank to bank across them.

Edward Paget-Tomlinson's drawing shows the wharf scene in 1900, where boats are lined up awaiting their loads. The railway was at a lower level behind the buildings. A wharf cottage and the unusual circular hovel were features of this location for many years.

In April 1923, a drift was completed from No. 2 (Uxbridge Colliery) to the surface near the basin. An overhead screen was constructed across the canal, which enabled boats to be loaded quickly from above. The old transhipping wharf became less important as boats queued up for the new screens.

When Cannock Chase Collieries closed in 1962, traffic on the Anglesey Branch dwindled. However, the old wharf was built up and tipping shoots added. Lorries brought coal from surviving local mines such as Rawnsley, and tipped the coal down the shoots into boats. This traffic ceased about 1970.

Angelsey Basin, coal chute and cottages.

Angelsey Basin, with a tug and several loaded day boats, and a coal chute top left.
The tug is *Helen,* in the service of Leonard Leigh Ltd.

B is for Blast Furnace

The principles of the smelting process that extracted iron from ironstone had been established long before the Birmingham Canal came into existence. Charcoal, then coke mixed with limestone, formed part of the basic ingredients that resulted in the manufacture of pig iron. Extraction of iron from its ores has been carried of centuries. Wherever these ores were found close to the surface, means were devised for the process. At first the method of iron extraction involved the bloomery. The fuel comprised charcoal; and water power came to be used to provide the necessary blasts of air that were required to raise the temperature of the fire.

Iron was worked in the West Midlands using bloomeries from medieval times. Production of iron by this method was extremely limited, however. With the blast furnace, production improved. Charcoal remained a basic fuel, and demand for charcoal encouraged a related industry of the charcoal burner. During the seventeenth century, the water power of local rivers such as the Stour and Tame was harnessed to not only provide the blast for furnaces, but also the forges that worked the iron up into bar iron, which was the basic commodity for sale.

The high temperatures within the furnace were achieved by creating a mechanical blast that forced air through the fire to enhance the combustion. Early furnaces were square in

Edward Paget-Tomlinson often used photographs to provide inspiration for the drawing. This is the Blast Furnaces scene that was used in this instance.

form, but these were later replaced by conical brick furnaces, held together by iron hoops. As technology improved iron manufacture, many cost saving devices were employed. Heating the blast and capturing the waste gases added extra plant that surrounded the basic structure.

The Black Country was fortunately endowed with rich supplies of coal, ironstone and limestone. A number of furnaces was established to smelt the local ores, and the canal played an integral part in moving these minerals to the furnace site. Blast furnaces, therefore, were common canal side features, particularly during the nineteenth century when the trade was at its height.

By the 1850s, the greatest number of working blast furnaces were to be found in this region. Statistics published for this period record that the total figure of extant furnaces exceeded 180. They were to be found alongside the banks of the Birmingham, Dudley, Stourbridge, Stourbridge Extension and Wyrley & Essington Canals.

The illustration is believed to be of the Capponfield Furnaces. It is redrawn from a photograph filed among the Springvale collection in the Wolverhampton Archives. The original Capponfield Furnaces had been established before 1820 on part of the Capponfield Colliery. The old line of the BCN passed through the colliery, and the furnaces were established near the northern bank. Since they were placed on the towpath side, a basin provided the connection with the canal.

William Aston, and later John Bagnall & Sons, was included amongst the proprietors of these furnaces, which came to be three in number. Local deposits of ironstone were used, but these were later supplemented with other ores from further afield. Bagnalls sold the furnaces to Alfred Hickman, who re-let them to T & I Bradley. There was a complete rebuild in 1901, when the railway sidings were extended, and two new iron-cased furnaces erected.

The photograph on which the drawing was based almost certainly dates from 1901 or later and appears to be taken from the first of two roving bridges. The BCN Bradley Loop is behind the cameraman, and the railway bridge that carried the line from Stourbridge to Wolverhampton is off camera to the right. The two basins, although close together, were originally constructed for different purposes. The far basin was made to serve the first furnaces, the other to meet a tramway from local mines.

From this viewpoint, the incline that carried the charge up to the furnace mouth is seen in the centre of the picture. A railway siding was located near its base. This image shows piles of pig iron stacked in front of the furnace. The day boat in the far basin appears to be loaded with slack, whilst that in the near basin had a finer material on board.

Iron was produced in a saleable commodity called pig iron. Pig iron varied in quality, and that quality was the result of the iron ores used and the mode of smelting. Black Country ironmasters did not just use local ores, but mixed the ores with others taken from elsewhere. Both canal and railway transport became a key factor in the import of ores and ironstone from other regions. There was an important trade in ores from Cumberland and Lancashire, ironstone from Derbyshire, North Staffordshire, Northamptonshire, Oxfordshire and Warwickshire.

Pig iron went on to be worked up into many forms. That transformation took place in the ironworks, many of which were placed close to the furnaces to reduce transport costs. Coal was needed in large quantities, partly for the puddling furnaces that converted the pig iron to wrought iron, and partly for the steam engines that drove the rolling mills and hammers. In this way iron was shaped into useful forms such as rods, bars, rails and sheets. These were then sold on for general use, such as railway track or building purposes or for further working up into useful products. Pig iron also was sold on for foundry use, where all forms of cast iron products might be made. These included products for domestic use such as pots and pans, but also items for specialist needs such as the casting required for the engineering trade.

Pig iron, wrought iron and castings were all significant cargoes in the hold of narrow boats navigating the Birmingham Canal network.

C is for Coseley Tunnel

The illustration shows the northern portal of Coseley Tunnel. The house above it was actually in Ivyhouse Lane, which passes above the tunnel mouth. Coseley Tunnel has a long and complicated history. It was, when completed in 1837, the only tunnel on the main line between Birmingham and Wolverhampton. The towpath on either side was constructed to the design of Thomas Telford who engineered the shorter route between these two towns. Construction work on the tunnel was authorised in 1835 and was completed on 6 November 1837. The new tunnel was an essential link in Telford's improvements to the canal that shortened the main line. A significant saving in distance was achieved by this simple cut. Boats had hitherto travelled through Bradley to reach Coseley. Now this older waterway was reduced to a secondary route.

When work started on Coseley Tunnel, Telford was dead and the task of finishing the work left to his successors. Yet Telford had accomplished much in his final years and when he died in 1834, was probably worn out. Between 1824 and 1834, he had undertaken the engineering and surveying of the BCN New Main Line, the Birmingham & Liverpool Junction Canal, works for the united Ellesmere & Chester Canal (Ellesmere Port and the Middlewich Branch) and three projects for the Trent and Mersey Canal (Harecastle Tunnel, Hall Green Branch and Wardle Branch). Such projects were not without their difficulties.

John Price & Son produced many postcard views of the Black Country including this view of the northern portal of Coseley Tunnel.

Coseley Canal Tunnel. Length, ¼ mile.

John Price & Son's Picture Post Cards. No. 76.

The problems of the Shelmore Embankment (Birmingham & Liverpool Junction Canal) have been well reported in canal histories. Less well reported were the troubles of making the Weaver Embankment for the Middlewich Branch.

Whilst Coseley Tunnel had a towpath on each side, the eastern one is now the only one in use.
Brenda Ward

Coseley Tunnel could have had a very different look if the original plans had been successful. Today this tunnel is 360 yards long, but it may well have been longer. An Act of Parliament authorised in 1794 originally sanctioned Coseley Tunnel. It was the same act that sanctioned the construction of the Walsall Canal. The new waterway was to be called the Bloomfield & Deepfield Cut. The contractors started at both ends. A waterway was cut from Deepfield Junction towards Ivyhouse Lane, whilst a second was made from the Bloomfield end. Both arms were in place by 1798, but not connected up. There were construction problems at the Bloomfield end; the contractors had great difficulty cutting this part. Eventually work ceased, although both ends were used as part of the navigation to serve collieries and ironstone mines.

It is possible to make out horse roads leading up to Ivyhouse Lane and the high bridge, which carries Central Drive over the canal. An earlier tunnel would, almost certainly, have lacked a towpath and these provisions would have had to be made. The southern portal may have been intended to start somewhere near the high bridge. The southern approach is made through a steeply graded cutting, and it is quite a climb to the top. Fairly recently, steps were put in to provide access to School Road, but previously the only access point was from Central Drive.

The Deepfield Cut served a variety of different industries, which included the Priorsfield Furnaces and Foundry, and there were a couple of side branches that provided access to mines and brickworks. One to the mines became known as the 'Deepfields Branch', whilst the other was called 'Hurst Hill Branch'.

SOUTH END OF COSELEY TUNNEL AND GROUNDS OF SUMMER HOUSE INN

Postcards were often quite decorative, here enhancing the view of the southern portal of Coseley Tunnel.

D is for Daw End, Dock and Day Boat

The letter D is the prefix to many features connected with the BCN. This drawing is a triple helping of Ds. It represents a day boat on a dock beside the Daw End Canal.

The Day Boat was once very common on the BCN. Often made of wood, these basic vessels were the work horses of the coal and iron industry. They carried coal from the mines to the furnaces, foundries and factories with often only a rudimentary protection for the steerer. Early boats were fashioned out of oak with elm bottoms, but BCN day boats were commonly made from cheaper materials such as pine. A number of boats were metal, and the BCN gauging registers refer to 'open iron' almost as frequently as 'open wood'.

A large fleet of day boats plied the waters of the BCN. They required regular maintenance, and a number of boatyards were established beside the canal for their construction and maintenance. Most the larger carrying firms such as John Whitehouse & Sons, Fellows Morton & Co and later coal carriers that included W H Bowater had their own yards. George Ryder Bird was an example of a boat builder turned carrier. But family firms who eked a living from the trade ran many more yards.

Peter Keay was one such builder who first established a yard beside the canal at Daw End after the First World War. He was later to have yards at Pratt's Bridge and Carl Street, Bloxwich, and it is his last yard at Carl Street for which he is best remembered.

The drawing shows a boat on the dock at Peter Keay's yard beside the Daw End Canal. The canal through Daw End between the wars remained a busy waterway for coal traffic. Boats from the Cannock Chase Coalfield passed down the Daw End Canal and through the Rushall Locks to firms such as the GEC at Witton.

The canal first served Daw End in 1800, when the branch that bears its name was constructed from Catshill Junction. It formed part of the Wyrley & Essington Canal that connected Wolverhampton with the Coventry Canal at Huddlesford. The early traffic on the waterway comprised mainly limestone, which was sent from Hay Head, the Linley and Winterley Limeworks. Later, bricks from the brickworks at Aldridge were also carried.

BCN day boats at the Black Country Living Museum, 2008. Compare this scene to that on page 75 which shows the same location when the lime kilns were in use. *Brenda Ward*

The Brawn family were important carriers on the Daw End Canal, as they were involved with both the brick and limestone trade. Brawn's Bridge is a lasting reminder of their long time relationship with the waterway.

The BCN became responsible for the Daw End Branch in 1840 when the Wyrley & Essington Canal Company merged with the Birmingham Canal Company. The BCN was keen to forge new links with the Wyrley & Essington, and one such link was the Rushall Canal.

Ken Keay's boat dock near Winterley Bridge, Ken having taken over his father's business in later years. The dock had three slipways which enabled six boats to be worked on.
Edwards Collection

With the completion of the Rushall canal in 1847, the Daw End Branch was upgraded to a through route to the Tame Valley Canal. Mining developments on Cannock Chase during the 1850s led to an increase in coal traffic on the canal, which was augmented through the opening of mines such as Walsall Wood and Leighswood near Aldridge.

Daw End is an example of the wooden boat building yard, which once prevailed in various spots along the canal bank, providing the requirement for new craft and boat maintenance. In addition to these, there were also the iron boat makers who also made boilers and tanks as part of their business. They too were once part of the local canal boat building scene.

Today, all the mines have closed, but the Daw End Canal remains for the boaters who have a thriving boatyard at Longwood.

Until 1847, the Daw End Branch ended here at Longwood - the terminus now forming the moorings of Longwood Boat Club. *Brenda Ward*

Jim Arnold on CEA butty no: 2207 loaded with slack near Bromford Lane. *Graham Guest*

Ken Keay's yard at Carl Street, Bloxwich (after he had moved from Daw End). The wood laid out on the trestles was the start of his boat *Linguist*. The date is probably mid 1970s (the car registration dates it as August 1973 at the very earliest).   *Gordon Thompson*

E is for Engine Aqueduct and Arm

In order to explain the history of the Engine Arm (or branch) and the aqueduct, it is important to look back at some of the factors that were responsible for its construction.

Smethwick has had a long association with the waterways. The original Birmingham Canal passed through the district, bringing coal from the Wednesbury mines into Birmingham. It was a canal fashioned to the designs of James Brindley, and the making of the waterway was not without problems.

Had Brindley's original plan, of 1767, been adopted, we would have seen a very different canal from that which exists today. It was suggested that a tunnel through the hillside be constructed at the 453 ft, or Birmingham level as it is known today. This tunnel would have commenced on the east side of Spon Lane, run under Roebuck Lane, and finished at a spot near the Blue Gates. It would have followed a very similar course to the present Birmingham Level Canal. A start was made sinking the tunnel shafts, but quicksand was encountered and work on the new tunnel was abandoned.

The canal proprietors quickly convened, and it was decided to build the canal over the hillside, rising by six locks and then descending again by six locks. It was this decision that was to later have a dramatic effect on the Smethwick landscape as successive canal engineers advocated ways of reducing the levels of the waterway.

The initial solution that created 12 locks on the line from the Wednesbury collieries, and nine on the main line to Wolverhampton, was to prove very unsatisfactory for two main reasons. The first was the unnecessary lockage that constantly delayed traffic on the canal. The second was the extremely short summit level, where supplies of water were limited.

Reservoirs were constructed at Smethwick and Titford, and these provided the main water supply. Soon, these reservoirs proved unequal to the task and steam engines were provided to pump water back to the top of the locks. Smeaton was employed to examine the canal route and reported on the supply of water from available streams and from the mine engines that pumped water into the canal. His report came to influence the proprietors of the canal for improvement.

The summit level was greatly increased in length when the top three locks of each flight were removed between 1789 and 1790. Navvies worked hard to cart away the earth and spoil that reduced the summit down to 473 feet, and left a deep cutting through the hillside between Smethwick and Spon Lane.

It was a remarkable feat of engineering, which was supervised by BCN engineers Bull & Bough. They managed to take down the summit level 18ft without serious disruption to trade. In fact they used the working canal to move spoil to places where the canal had already subsided through mining operations. They also used innovative technology such as portable steam engines for pumping water, and horse gins to draw spoil out of the excavations.

The new works involved major alterations to the courses of the feeders that supplied water into the summit level. Two engines had been provided to back-pump water at Smethwick and Spon Lane. The channels from these engines fed into the canal above the sixth and seventh lock respectively. The Spon Lane Engine became redundant when the summit was lowered, but Smethwick (1779) Engine took on a more important role. This engine now had to back-pump water for the two pairs of locks that now comprised the Smethwick Flight. A new feeder was constructed, in 1790, from the Smethwick Engine to pass water into the canal above the third pair of locks. It is likely that this feeder was made navigable to take coal up to the engine. Meanwhile, traffic on the canal continued to increase and in 1804 a second engine was provided to assist the first. This feeder must be considered as the first Engine Arm.

Thomas Telford suggested further improvements, which not only resulted in the making of a new and deeper canal cutting, but also in the complete change of the water supply to the canal system. It was out of these improvements carried out between 1826 and 1829 that the Engine Aqueduct came into being.

A new reservoir was constructed at Rotton Park between 1826 and 1827, which received water from the Rowley Hills via Titford Reservoir and fed it back into the canal system as required. A culvert was constructed from Rotton Park to join the 473ft level at Smethwick. From Rabone Lane to the canal junction, this culvert was made as a navigable canal, which became known as the Engine Branch. The new Engine Branch appears to have been made close to, if not along, the earlier feeder. However, the junction with the canal may have been a few yards to the north.

Engine Aqueduct and Arm, the focal point of the BCNS bonfire rally for many years.
BCNS Archives

Part of the works involved the construction of an aqueduct over Telford's new canal at the 453ft level. It comprises an iron trough supported on a cast iron laced arch, with brick and stone abutments. This decorative aqueduct, designed by Telford, was completed in May 1829. The new Engine Branch brought coal to the two Boulton & Watt pumping engines in Bridge Street, which continued to circulate water between the 453ft and 473ft levels.

Casualties of the new improvements were the Smethwick Reservoirs. They ceased to be used as a water supply from 1833, and were subsequently abandoned. The site of the Great Smethwick Reservoir was later covered by streets and houses, whilst industry soon established itself along the banks of the Engine Arm feeder. This included ironworks, foundries, screw and rivet manufactories.

The junction with the Wolverhampton Level is made at right angles. The Engine Arm then passes under a brick towpath bridge before crossing the Birmingham Level by the Telford Aqueduct. There is then a right angle turn that brings the waterway on to a similar course to the Birmingham Level. A single towpath follows the navigable part to the end. Facing the aqueduct, on the opposite side to the towpath, was a wharf that first served an ironworks, but was later used by Smethwick Corporation. There is one side bridge that crossed the basin into the Valor Company Stamping Works. The canal then passes under Bridge Street before terminating near Rabone Lane. Here the waterway changes into a narrow culvert for the rest of its length.

The old beam engines ceased to be used after 1892, when they were replaced by the Brasshouse Lane Engine. They remained here until 1897, when the buildings were demolished. The older beam engine, of 1779, was moved to Ocker Hill maintenance depot where it was available for inspection by those interested in the Boulton & Watt design. With the closure by British Waterways of Ocker Hill, the engine was moved to the Birmingham Science Museum, where it stood in a purpose made engine hall beside Whitmore's Arm. With the closure of this museum, the engine was moved again to Millennium Point.

The engine house site, at Smethwick was excavated during 1984, and is now a Scheduled Monument. The Aqueduct was restored in 1985 and is also a Scheduled Monument.

The Engine Arm today remains virtually intact, although the adjacent premises have long ceased to use the canal for transport. Access is possible from the Aqueduct end and Bridge Street. Some important surviving features are located at the end of the branch. These include a Lime Wharf, an old Malthouse (complete with timber hoist) and the Coal Merchant's Yard. It is well worth the walk.

Extract from the 1911/1919 distance tables:
Engine Branch

Towpath Side	Canal	Offside
		Smethwick Corporation Wharf
		Smethwick Foundry
		Patent Rivet Works
Anchor Ironworks		
Valor Co		
		BCN Engine Wharf
	Bridge St	
		BCN Engine Wharf
		Victoria Foundry
Credenda Works		
		Eagle Works

Soap Works
Lusty's Timber Yard
Hamstead Officials Coal Co's Wharf
S D Williams & Co Lime Wharf
Malthouse Wharf

BCN French Walls
(Engine Top Wharf)   End of Branch
                       (3.5 furlongs)

The Birmingham Canal Navigation Society assisted with subsequent improvements made to the arm, which included the making of a turning basin at the end of the arm. The section east of Bridge Street North was converted by British Waterways into residential moorings.

1990 – Engine Arm aqueduct taking the Engine Arm over Telford's 'new' main line. As well as serving industry, the Engine Arm was also part of the BCN water supply system. *Stanley Holland*

The Engine Arm was very much hemmed in by industry although it had only one basin off it, the towpath bridge of which can be seen in the distance. Here in 1978 a pleasure boat is possibly reversing up the arm; until recently there was no place to turn at the end! *Stanley Holland*

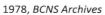

1978, BCNS Archives

Two views of the end of the Engine Arm where the feeder from Edgbaston reservoir entered. The moorings are on the left opposite the Malthouse (referred to on page 34).

F is for Farmer's Bridge Locks

It is common to find groups of locks named after places and areas where they are located. It is unusual to find them named after a bridge. The name Farmer's Bridge is derived from the occupation bridge on James Farmer's land that crossed the Newhall Branch. That bridge is long gone but the name has survived - in the form of a canal junction, ticket office and a flight of locks.

Farmer's Bridge became important in canal terms when a political compromise decided the route of a new canal. The Birmingham & Fazeley Canal had been promoted to exploit the rich coal reserves at Wednesbury through a line that united the proposed canal with the Coventry and Oxford canals. The new canal originally intended to turn off through Lozells, and make its way through the Tame Valley to Wednesbury. The Birmingham Canal also intended to tap these mines by an extension of their waterway. The Government of the day decided on the compromise that led to diversion of the Birmingham & Fazeley to join the Birmingham Canal Navigation at Mrs Farmer's Bridge. The waters of the old Birmingham Canal were then used to reach a detached portion of the Birmingham & Fazeley Canal. The Act of 1783 which authorised the building of the Farmer's Bridge Locks was followed in 1784 by the act that permitted the merger

Farmer's Bridge Locks, (Lock 8 from Junction) Newhall Street.
The Birmingham & Fazeley Canal descended through 13 locks to the Hospital Pound. Most of the length came to be lined with a number of different industries. In this view, the canal is surrounded by the Elkington Works, where electroplating was first developed by Elkington and Mason, and was used to create artistic items. The side bridge on the left spanned the entrance to Whitmore's Arm where the wharf for Elkingtons factory was located. In the distance and in the shadows of the buildings, can be seen the arches of Newhall Street Bridge.

Looking down the Farmer's Bridge lock flight from Lock 1, early 1900s.
Bob May Collection

of the Birmingham Canal Navigations and the Birmingham & Fazeley Canal.

Construction of the locks then followed, with Thomas Sheasby appointed contractor. The surrounding land was still mainly rural but factories and works gradually came to line the waterway. A number of wharves and a few basins were constructed to serve the industry that developed there.

The thirteen locks which join Hospital Pound (372 ft) with the Birmingham Level (453ft) at Farmer's Bridge formed part of the Birmingham & Fazeley route. After 1790, this piece of waterway became an essential link in the canal network. Carriers' boats pied to and fro with merchandise and iron goods and numerous coal boats passed down the flight with fuel destined for the many factories located in the Aston and Digbeth districts. The traffic became so busy that night working was eventually instituted.

A feature of the canal north of Newhall Street was an old gas lamp bracket that survived until recent times fixed to a wall near the Science Museum. With recent redevelopment of the building adjoining the towpath, this bracket has disappeared.

There was one rolling mill in Water Street that pre-dated the Farmer's Bridge Locks. Charles Twigg, James Pickard and Sampson Freeth had leased land in 1779 from Henrieta and William Inge and had established two mills for the grinding and boring of gun barrels and the rolling of metals. A Newcomen engine was utilised to provide the power.

The mill was carried on by James Pickard and then passed to Muntz and Purdon. In Muntz's time it is recorded as a copper and brass rolling mill. It was at this works that George Frederick Muntz started making Muntz's Metal, a brass alloy with a high content of zinc. This metal was particularly suited to sheathing ships' wooden bottoms.

The Water Street Mill was located on the towpath side near the first lock. In 1807, the Phoenix Foundry was erected on the other side of the bottom lock and utilised the wharf space of the side pound there. Phoenix Foundry was set up by John Walker, but by 1812 was worked by George Jones.

There was a branch canal, which came off above the eight lock known as Whitmore's Arm. The origin of the name Whitmore is derived from William Whitmore who had a foundry in Lionel Street. William Whitmore senior was engineer to the making of the Southern Stratford Canal. His association with William James was no doubt an influential factor in his appointment.

Farmer's Bridge Locks, near Saturday Bridge (Lock 5 from Junction). The extensive Pen Factory, whose original premises were in Charlotte Street, was extended across the canal, with newer premises in Fleet Street. Steel pen manufacture was once an important Birmingham trade with factories in various parts of the city.

Initially Whitmore's Arm was a short length built for Caroline Colmore and served a non–ferrous metal rolling mill.

William James planned to build an internal port near the Sandpits that would be linked to one of his railway schemes. Whitmore was involved with the extension of the arm under Caroline Street and George Street and the turn around to Newhall Hill, where it finished, although there was an intention to take it further.

Whitmore's Arm generated a variety of canal traffic, and the Colmore family no doubt benefited from the lucrative rents that canal-side property once brought. During the nineteenth century, the arm had a copper works, a glassworks, a nickel and cobalt refinery, a timber yard and, of course, a coal yard.

The illustration shows a scene at the turn of the century that looks down on the seventh lock from the sixth, above. The basin on the left once served Shipton's Timber Yard, while the bridge over the Whitmore's Arm can be seen lower down the flight. The buildings that line the canal on either side belonged to Elkingtons who were electroplaters. Their premises extended up to, and across, Whitmore's Arm at this time. This property was on a long lease from the executors of the Colmore (Newhall) Estates. The buildings on the right were on canal company land.

The drawing shows the two arches of Newhall Street Bridge, which are still there today. Beyond Newhall Street Bridge was Shelton's Timber Yard and Water Street Power Station. Both premises at one time or another were responsible for important canal trade.

Today, Farmer's Bridge Locks fulfil mainly a recreational role. Boaters regularly bring their boats up and down the flight. There are many walkers and enthusiastic joggers who pass along the towpath. Much has changed since the canal trade was at its height, but there is still much to retain the interest. Victorian and Georgian buildings mingle with modern structures. Some bridges such as Newhall Street have changed little and the cobbles, worn by the shoes of countless boat horses, bear testament to a former age.

Farmer's Bridge locks from above, showing locks 5-8 running parallel to Fleet Street.
BCNS Archives

The bottom lock of the Farmer's Bridge flight with hotel pair butty *Ellesmere* entering the lock. The cavernous bridge of the Great Western Railway's Birmingham Snow Hill station crosses the flight in the background.
Ray Shill

1987 - Cambrian Wharf, with the Birmingham canal coming in from Old Turn Junction to the left, the former Newhall Branch leaving bottom centre, and above that, Farmer's Bridge top lock. *Stanley Holland*

On the right, Cambrian Wharf, leading to the now blocked off Newhall Branch which extended for about ¼ mile, and to the left, the top lock of the Farmer's Bridge flight, the first of thirteen descending from the 453' Birmingham level. *Bob May Collection*

G is for Gas Street Basin

Gas Street Basin is the meeting place of two canals. It is here that the Worcester & Birmingham Canal joins the Birmingham Canal Navigations, and parts of both waterways make up what is known today as Gas Street Basin. It is a busy place where boats are constantly present. Tourists and the general public find it a popular place to visit. There are a number of canal side public houses and eating places which add to the attraction of the area.

Since the 1990s there have been many changes, though, with developments now out of use. The James Brindley Public House once busy with the supply of the drinks and food to the general public is presently closed. Boaters frequently plan their journeys to pass through the basin using nearby moorings for an overnight stop. It is also still a place for boaters who use the moorings beside the bar as home. Gas Street is also a place of contrasts where old meets new. A number of buildings have survived from the canal age. Old BCN and Worcester & Birmingham cottages blend with much newer structures. Planners consciously attempted to integrate the past with the present.

The BCN buildings in Gas Street (from Quayside Tower Car Park), 1990s. *Ray Shill*

Many people welcome the modern Gas Street image, and the changes have been seen as improvement rather that a past destroyed. It could have been all so very different. One plan of the 1950s threatened to destroy the waterway and turn the basin into an ornamental pool! Be thankful that option was never adopted.

For the historian, Gas Street has a complex history, and has seen at least six ages. The first age was one of development. Elements of the original Gas Street Basin formed part of Paradise Branch completed in 1773 for the Birmingham Canal Navigation. The terminal basins faced Paradise Street where the company offices were erected. The Paradise Branch was constructed through land belonging the King Edward's Grammar School and ended at Brick Kiln Croft, which belonged to Thomas Gooch. Surprisingly, or coincidentally, the later Digbeth Branch also terminated in the land of Thomas Gooch.

The canal to Brick Kiln Croft was completed about a year after the Newhall Branch was extended to a terminal basin at Newhall Ring. Birmingham thus had two termini for its canal.

During the next seventeen years, traffic on the BCN started to develop and Paradise Wharf became a busy place. Coal was the principal traffic, but iron goods and merchandise were also carried. In those days, Gas Street did not exist. The canal passed under Broad Street and then curved round to pass under Bridge Street to reach the Paradise Street Wharves. A boat yard was established on the offside of the curve, and boat building was carried on here for a number of years.

The second age began in 1790, when the Birmingham Canal was linked by the Fazeley Canal to the Coventry Canal. The BCN was no longer a dead end waterway serving the needs of Birmingham and the Black Country. It was now a link in a growing network of inland navigation. Carriers started to set up warehouses in Birmingham, and canalside property was eagerly sought by businessmen who relied on the canal for transport. Warehouses began to be established on the section between Broad Street and Bridge Street, and two private basins were constructed for the carriers boats calling there. One basin faced Broad Street opposite to King Edward's Place, the other was made parallel to a part of Broad Street, which was then called Islington. This second basin was usually known as Islington Basin.

This was also an age of canal expansion. The Worcester &

Gas Street Basin, IWA Rally 1969, and the by now gate-less Worcester Bar lock.   *Bob May Collection*

Birmingham Canal Bill was sanctioned by Parliament in 1791. Work started at the Birmingham end, and slowly construction proceeded towards Worcester. The Worcester & Birmingham Canal was separated from the BCN by a piece of land 84 yards long and 7ft 3in wide. There was no connection between the canals; all goods had to be transhipped across the bar.

The property at either end of the bar also became utilised. In 1804, wharf accommodation on the Bridge Street side was advertised for sale and became a carriers wharf. On the Broad Street side the Birmingham Timber Company had a large piece of land. The boat dock continued to be used, and by 1800 was occupied by George Ryder Bird.

Worcester Bar, with stop lock gates still in use, late 1940s.
Bob May Collection

The Dudley Canal proprietors were keen to carry coal from the Netherton mines into Birmingham, and with the completion of the canal to Selly Oak in 1798, were able to do so. Coal was first carried under the alias of the Netherton Coal Company who also subleased a piece of land from the Birmingham Timber Company. A basin was completed by 1803 and was wide enough at the top end to moor a narrow boat. This basin joined with the Worcester & Birmingham Canal a few yards south of the Bar. Essentially this basin functioned as a detached portion of the Dudley Canal. Dudley Canal Proprietors let wharf and warehouse space for coal merchants and carriers, but also retained a piece of wharf for public use.

The third canal age began in 1815 when the Worcester & Birmingham Canal was about to be finished and joined with the River Severn at Diglis. Parliament also authorised the breaching of the bar with a lock. The new bar lock was on the boat dock side, and with the construction of the lock all traces of the boatyard was obliterated. The reconstruction also affected the Timber Company, who chose to sell the yard and their adjacent property. The BCN Bar Lock cottage appears to date from this period.

Most of the early Worcester & Birmingham Canal warehouses were located near Holliday Street, but the land was gradually built up from Bridge Street, and a line of new warehouses and wharves established there.

A rough track from Broad Street to Holliday Street was used by carters and waggoners bringing and taking goods to the timber yard and the Islington & Netherton Canal Basin. It was intended to call this thoroughfare Netherton Street, but in 1817 John Gostling established a gasworks near the Netherton Basin and thereafter the road became known as Gas Street.

Working boats moored on both sides of Worcester Bar in the late 1960s.
In the foreground, Birmingham & Midland Canal Carrying Admiral Class motor boat *Collingwood* and Grand Union Canal Carrying Co. small Woolwich butty *Achilles*. *Bob May Collection*

The fourth age happened through railway competition, and begins after 1850. Canal carrying was still important, but some of the early carriers' warehouses at Broad Street, Islington & Netherton basins ceased to be used and were adopted by other industries. The two basins on either side of the bar served a boiler and engine manufactory, a lead works and a tube works.

This was perhaps the darkest time for Gas Street Basin as buildings completely lined the waterway. Even Broad Street Bridge had a row of buildings across it on both sides and the canal passed underneath in a virtual tunnel.

The fifth age began in 1920 with a decline in canal trade. Coal continued to be the most common traffic, but merchandise remained important. The Severn & Canal Carrying Company boats were daily visitors to the large canal warehouse in Bridge

Street. They were commonly seen lined up with other carriers on either side of the Worcester Bar, as is depicted in the drawing.

For many Brummies, Gas Street Basin was unseen and forgotten cocooned behind the tall buildings and walls that surrounded it. A gate in the Gas Street wall was a passport to another world that few people, other than boatmen, ventured into.

The bad winter of 1963 killed off many of the surviving canal carrying firms, but there was a new interest in canals dawning. Pleasure boating was increasing. People had more time for leisure pursuits, and boating became more popular. The 1970s heralded a new, and sixth age, where boaters regularly plied the canal network. During the 1980s and 1990s amenities have improved, and Gas Street Basin has been radically transformed into a pleasing place to be.

It is perhaps a pity that the warehouses were destroyed, but period buildings remain and still see use, even if it is in a different guise. At least they survive!

The road entrance to Gas Street Basin, with the BCN company offices (since demolished).

Bagging up coal - Jim Marshall and Ian Kemp, with *Comet* and *Betelgeuse*, 1973.   *Bob May Collection*

H is for Hockley Port

Hockley Port is located beside the Soho Loop on the BCN. It constitutes an arm and two basins and is chiefly used for residential moorings. Entrance to the arm and basin is through the side bridge that carries the towpath over the arm. The name Hockley Port is of comparatively recent origin and can be confusing to some who might expect a complex of docks and a heritage of large ships calling there.

In truth, Hockley Port was once a busy interchange point where goods were transferred between the Great Western Railway and the BCN. In those days it was known as Hockley Basin and the arm off the Soho Loop was called the Birmingham Heath Branch. When the railways were done with Hockley, a period of dereliction set in. Boaters used the two railway basins for cheap moorings and eventually the site was converted into residential moorings.

Survivors from a past age are the railway stables and related buildings. These are a reminder of the days when horses were common on our streets working the railway cartage service that served industry and the community.

Hockley Goods was established by the Great Western Railway in 1855 alongside their railway from Birmingham (Snow Hill) to Wolverhampton. Sidings were made to a new canal basin on the Birmingham Heath Branch at the same time. The canal was on higher ground, and a hydraulic wagon lift was installed to raise the wagons from Hockley Goods up to the basin level. The lift was placed beside All Saints Road , and the railway tracks passed under the road to reach the base of the lift.

The Great Western Railway owned a number of boats which plied between their basins and local works. Traffic was quite varied, but included nuts and bolts and copper strip. A GWR boat is depicted in the drawing. It is tied up outside the basin awaiting its next load. The Great Western Boats were quite colourful; Douglas Clayton recalls that their cabin livery was similar to their coaching stock painted in chocolate and cream. They were indeed a colourful contrast to the dark liveries of the boats owned by other railway companies.

Hockley ceased to be a railway interchange basin in 1958, although it is difficult to state the accurate date for closure. The occasional boat continued to call, but the general trade stopped in 1958. Hockley Goods remained open to rail traffic but, it too, closed - in 1967.

The Birmingham Heath (or Soho) Branch was completed in 1801. It was a short canal, about a quarter of a mile long, which left the Old Main Line of the BCN near Winson Green and terminated at Soho Wharf. It was constructed at the request of Matthew Boulton, who needed better canal facilities for the Soho Manufactory. Soho Wharf was chiefly used by coal merchants who used it to stack coal brought from Black Country and later Cannock Chase collieries. The branch also served a flint glass works, a rolling mill and a timber yard. Flint glass manufacture is normally associated with the Stourbridge area, but Birmingham also had number of flint glass works. Most were placed near to canals where they could receive sand and limestone essential to the manufacturing process.

In February 1865, two boatman were on a boat laden with a coal near at Soho Pool Wharf. Suddenly the boat surged forward taking them with it. They threw out ropes to men on the towpath, but none was able to render assistance. The boat sped on and was dragged towards a whirl pool that had appeared in the waterway. The two boatmen were terrified and did not know what to do. They might have jumped ashore, but feared that they might miss their footing and fall back into the canal.

As the boat was drawn into the whirlpool it struck the side heavily and the boatmen were able to scramble on to the towing path. The two men rapidly ran along the path as ground behind them fell into a deep chasm. It is a tale that might well have gripped the attention in a work of fiction, as the hero escaped in the nick of time. Both men were probably lucky to be alive.

1973 - Hockley Port was built as an interchange basin for the Great Western Railway, and subsequently has become a location for residential moorings.
BCNS Archives

The reason behind the calamity was probably poor workmanship by a railway contractor. In 1854, the Great Western Railway line from

Birmingham (Snow Hill) to Wolverhampton (Low Level) was opened for traffic. North of Hockley, the line went into a hundred yard tunnel which passed under the Birmingham Heath Branch.

On the day in question, the driver of the 4.11 from Wolverhampton noted water running down the side of the tunnel and onto the permanent way. As soon as he reached Hockley Station, the alarm was given and men were sent back to look at the damage. The trickle became a flood and soon a great body of water was running down towards Park Road. Walls were brought down and roads torn up by the force of the current. Railway workers laboured all night to repair the damage, but it was not until the next day the railway was reopened for traffic.

Hockley Port has become a flourishing mooring for leisure boaters. In recent years pleasure boats have become more conservative in style, but in 1976 the boat moored at Hockley Port were much more varied.

Soho was one of two places where the canal crossed over the GWR line to Wolverhampton, the other was at Wednesbury just north of Swan Village tunnel. The top end (120 yards) of the Soho Branch was officially abandoned in 1909. The Act enabled the Great Western Railway to widen their lines from Hockley to Winson Green and remove the tunnel.

The waterway was then cut back to a new terminus beside Lodge Road, which became the new Soho Wharf. Today this piece of canal is filled in and has been used as a scrap yard and later bus garage. The only part in water lies between Lodge Road and the Winson Green Loop and now forms part of Hockley Port.

I is for Indexing Station

The receipt of tolls was integral to the existence of any canal company. The cash raised through tolls provided the funds for maintenance, wages and the all important dividend for the shareholders.

A number of factors decided the toll paid. Amount, commodity and distance were combined together with mathematical calculation to determine the charge due. Unfortunately the magic formula was often complicated by variable factors which included the size and shape of the boat. In a truthful society, those that collected the tolls would have no problem taking the correct amount. But the intransigent nature of some canal carriers meant that the canal owners had to devise means of checking what was carried.

Every steerer navigating a canal, on passing the toll house, had to present the keeper with a written statement of the loading. On this statement was based the charges for the journey along the canal. The keeper, in turn, had to check the loading. The gauging rod was the common tool used by every toll keeper to check the veracity of the loading for any boat The simple process of setting the rod against the side of the boat determined, through the vessel's depth in the water, the tonnage carried. Metal graduated indexes fixed to either side of the vessel enabled the person using the gauging rod to obtain a reasonable tonnage estimate.

Most canals built from 1790 onwards have specific reference to the gauging of boats. Often the same wording is used. Some make specific reference to boat indexes. All have some fixed fine for abuse. The wording of the Wyrley & Essington Act, 1792, provides an example of one which gives specific reference to the index:

And for preventing disputes touching the Weight of Lading on board any Boat or other vessel passing on said Canal or Collateral Cuts, be it further enacted, that the masters or owners of all such Boats and other Vessels, shall and they are here required to fix on each side of their boat thereof respectively, correct indexes of Copper or Iron of such graduated dimensions, and such convenient height, as the said company of proprietors shall from time to time direct, so that the true weight of lading on board may at all times be ascertained and shewn.

Many canal acts have a separate clause for Gauging. The Wyrley & Essington Act had wording common to most acts of its time:

And it be further enacted, that the owner or master of every such boat or vessel shall permit and suffer the same to be gauged or measured, at the expense of the said Company of Proprietors, or such person or persons as shall be appointed by them for that purpose, provided that no such boat or other vessel shall be gauged or measured more than four times in any one year; and every owner, master or other person having the rule or command of any such boat or vessel, who shall refuse to permit and suffer the same to be gauged or measured as aforesaid, shall for every such offence, forfeit and pay a sum not exceeding five pounds.

The reference to Gauging, in this second instance with a capital G rather than a small g, was the physical measurement of a boat's depth with different loads. These measurements produced what is commonly known as a gauging table, but they may also have assisted the correct placing of the boat index.

Canal companies had gauging docks where these tasks could be carried out, which were frequently near other canal or river junctions. The Trent & Mersey Company had a dock at Fradley near the junction with the Coventry Canal, while the Staffordshire & Worcester Canal had a dock at Stourport.

Little is, however, known about the early gauging policies of the Birmingham Canal Navigations. The wording of their original Act (1768) states that it was lawful for a toll collector on the BCN to stop and detain a boat to weigh, measure, gauge or cause to be weighed, measured or gauged all such goods, ware and merchandise as shall be therein contained. The BCN staff had the authority to unload the boat and weigh the contents with consequential delay to its journey. There was nothing in any of their subsequent acts until 1811 that related to indexes or authority to Gauge (in a dock).

The 1811 BCN Act admitted that the authority to detain a boat caused expense and inconvenience and should not be resorted to unless in cases of necessity. Instead, it was made lawful to charge the weight according to the Gauge of such boat or the graduated index thereon. The change of wording enabled the BCN to accept a gauging certificate from another company, but did not give it the authority to Gauge boats. The company may have been wary of offending the short distance traders who made up the bulk of their revenue.

Matters were further clarified after the 1835 BCN Act passed Parliament. This was the crucial act that gave the BCN powers to gauge boats. A person was to be appointed to:

gauge, weigh and measure any such boats and shall from time to time enter in a book to be kept for that purpose the particulars of the measurement and weight thereof and also at the expense of the said company, affix on such boat an iron or other metal plate containing the gauge number thereof.

Thus the way was set for the BCN to set up a Gauging dock. The site chosen was at Smethwick on Telford's new Island Line. The 1841 census refers to the dock as the Smethwick Indexing Station which suggests from its title that it was used to fit indexes to the sides of the boats (the 'wet-inch' system). Smethwick may have also compiled gauging tables for boats, although none of these early records appear to have survived.

The Index Station at Smethwick was located next to the toll house and offices, and underneath a footbridge that crossed the canal. It comprised two piers and a central channel. Through traffic passed either side. Smethwick Indexing Station was open to the air and apparently devoid of buildings.

The subsequent canal mergers and additional mileage added to the BCN between 1840 and 1863 put a strain on the Smethwick Indexing Station. It also appears that not all boats were gauged. Many of the coal boats were exempt from weighing. A change in BCN policy, in 1872, led to the revision of the instruction for gauging. It now applied to all vessels and the Indexing Station became the Gauging Station. Permission was given to improve Smethwick and build a new gauging station at Tipton.

Indexing did not prevent the prevailing practice of long weight where coal, ironstone and iron were weighed with an allowance for loss. Long weight may add a hundred weight or more to the value of the ton measure. It was mentioned that as much as 2688 lbs

The twin basins of Tipton Indexing station allowed two boats to be gauged at once, although here only the left hand basin door is open with the stern of the boat being gauged visible.

to the ton was allowed, although it was commonly 2400 lbs to the ton. The customer in this way did not suffer loss in transfer, but the supplier effectively funded the extra material to their own cost. As coal became more expensive to mine, coal suppliers were particularly vocal in having a more accurate measure of weight. The Birmingham Canal Navigation met this request through changing the method from the system of fixing boat indexes to the effective calibration of a boat.

In 1873, the Gauging Station at Tipton opened its doors. The work was carried out in two covered basins above the Top Factory Lock. Each basin was one boat's length. At Smethwick Station, the piers were lengthened and widened and covered with a building similar to Tipton. Although there was only one through basin, it was two boats in length, and therefore could deal with the same amount of boats as Tipton. Both stations were provided with hydraulic cranes.

Caggy Stevens' tug waits at the top of Factory Three Locks whilst the boats it has towed are locked down. This is 1966 and the indexing station has closed. The Inspector's house is visible.
Waterways Images

The purpose of these stations was to produce a gauging table for each boat A copy of each table was then bound with others in books and deposited at each toll house for the reference of the collectors there.

Gauging weights were supposed to be accurate to the ton, but there was some mention in BCN records of other sets that still favoured longweight measurement! At the same time there was a prevailing country wide opinion to eliminate the longweight practice. A new weights and measures act came into force in 1879 and the 1893 BCN Act regarding tolls also made inroads into removing the practice. The revised canal rates clearly registered a dissent from those who still managed to get around the system A letter written to the Birmingham Daily Post by George Crowther of Chance Brothers, glassmakers, Spon Lane (23 November 1892) refers to the reduction in the present standard weight of 2400lbs to the ton to the Imperial Standard of 2240lbs per ton. His complaint was the additional cost of the coal and slack at a time of foreign competition in the window glass trade.

The reissue of gauging tables from this period would indicate a tightening up of the system and from then until trade declined true gauging weights by the 'dry-inch' system were ensured, even if it might have been a nail in the bulk coal carrying coffin.

Smethwick stopped gauging boats in the early 1920s. The buildings were pulled down in 1945, and some of the brickwork was used to fill the central channel. Tipton was used until about 1959. The drawing shows the interior of the Tipton Gauging Station when it was busy gauging boats.

Some fifty years have passed since the Tipton Gauging station building ceased to be used and since closure has been let by British Waterways and their successors, CRT for general industrial use. The station building was listed as grade II. There were plans in 2007 to convert the premises into houses, but the Dudley Canal Trust was also keen to use the building as a base for the tunnel trip boats. Neither has happened and the buildings remain as they were.

During this time, there was also an application to English Heritage to have the building reclassified as grade II*. The basic reason for this request was to recognise the new method of gauging employed. In particular the abandonment of the system that allowed both measurement in short weight and long weight and the standard measurement becoming the accurate 20 cwt to a ton. English Heritage did not consider this step as significant enough to change the classification and so the building remains listed as grade II.

Tipton Gauging Station more recently.   *Brenda Ward*

J is for *James Loader*

The letter J has several BCN connections. It could be J for Josher, which is the term of endearment often given to a boat owned by Fellows, Morton & Clayton. This is derived from Joshua Fellows, one of the firm's founders, who commenced his carrying career working for his father, James, on the BCN. J can also stand for Joey boat, which is the local name for the un-powered day boat once so common on the BCN. Joey is said to be a corruption of Joseph and the term is attributed to either Joseph Lovekin or Joseph Worsey, who both built day boats for the BCN.

There were surprisingly few canal features which began with J, although there still is a James Bridge Aqueduct and there was a James Bridge Colliery. Jubilee Colliery, West Bromwich also sent coal by canal, but this was only done after the coal had travelled a mile from the colliery to the wharf at Smethwick. There were some successful iron masters named Jones who had furnaces and ironworks dotted around the BCN, but not a single blast furnace ever had a name that started with a J !

The *James Loader* was a BCN tug, of wooden construction, built by Worseys of Walsall in 1946 for the coal factor and merchant, Leonard Leigh Limited. This tug was named after his son, James Loader Leigh. The tug *Christopher James* built by Spencer Abbot, Salford Bridge was named after another son.

James Loader commenced service in 1947 and worked for Leighs until 1963. The main duty was to bring trains of coal boats to and from the collieries on the Cannock Chase, a duty which is depicted in the drawing. *James Loader* is seen passing along a stretch of the Cannock Extension Canal hauling a number of loaded coal boats.

Whilst *Christopher James* was similar to the *James Loader,* it was built by Spencer Abbot, by Les Allen.

Most Cannock Chase collieries had some form of canal loading facilities for the boats. Originally this traffic was horse worked, but after 1920 tugs became a common site on the northern BCN fetching coals from Cannock Chase to the power station and many other canal side factories, ironworks and mills. Here they had a particular advantage over the motorboat and butty, where a number of coal boats could be towed without the impediment of delay by locks.

Leonard Leigh owned a large fleet of boats, most of which were traditional narrow boats. They handled both coal and rubbish, but coal was the most important revenue earner. Leigh competed for this trade with a host of carriers, which included firms such as H S Pitt, S E Barlow, Spencer Abbott, D N Stevenson, T & S Element and T Boston.

Leigh's coal carrying business could amount to over 5000 tons a month, much of which was arranged by contract for specific periods. The following is a list of one month's figures:

September 1934
Details of Leonard Leigh Coal Traffic
HQ Wharf Street, Hockley

Tons	Colliery	Destination
119	Aldridge	GEC Witton
25	Brownhills	Winfields Mill, Gibsons Arm, Birmingham
1547	Cannock & Rugeley	Nechells Power station
32	Cannock & Rugeley	Browning Street Wharf
122	Cannock & Rugeley	Freeth St. Rolling Mills, Birmingham
207	Cannock & Rugeley	Lion Tube Works, Wednesfield
91	Cannock & Rugeley	Phoenix Tube Works, W Bromwich
87	Cannock Chase	Junction Foundry, Pleck Walsall
88	Cannock Chase	Lion Tube Works, Wednesfield
30	Cannock Chase	Sandwell IW, Smethwick
346	Cannock Chase	Smethwick Power Station
89	Cannock Chase	Stock & Co, Gas St, Birmingham

297	Hamstead	GEC Witton
263	Hamstead	D Taylor, Whitmore Arm, Birmingham
264	Hamstead	Tubes Ltd, Rocky Lane, Aston
175	Hamstead	Tubes Ltd, Bromford Lane, Erdington
51	Hamstead	Walsall Glue Works, Green Lane
168	Holly Bank	Mond Gasworks, Tipton
60	Holly Bank	Tipton Gasworks
29	Icknield Port Wharf	GEC Witton
26	Mid Cannock	Icknield Port Wharf, Birmingham
158	Mid Cannock	D Taylor, Whitmore Arm, Birmingham
55	Mid Cannock	United Wire, Adderley Street, Birmingham
61	Sandwell Park	Tubes Ltd, Rocky Lane, Aston
28	Walsall Wood	Coombeswood Tube Works, Halesowen
187	Walsall Wood	Walsall Power Station

Nationalisation of the coal industry led to a process of rationalisation and closure of uneconomic coalmines. Many mines on Cannock Chase were shut down between 1960 and 1970 and most of the canal trade had been lost to the railways and roads before that. Subsidence had also seriously affected the Cannock Extension Canal, and it was decided to close the waterway north of the A5 in 1963 even though Mid Cannock and Cannock Wood collieries were still working at this date. Few mines remained with canal side connections; time was running out for the tug and coal boat on the northern BCN.

In 1963, *James Loader* was sold to Peter Freakley, who refurbished her and fitted a Gardner 2L engine. The tug has remained in private ownership ever since. Only 16 years of the boat's life was spent in revenue earning service.

K is for Kenrick Foundry

The Birmingham Canal Navigation has changed in many ways since the time of the working boat. Many of the older canal side buildings have been pulled down or modified for new roles. Very few are still in use for the purpose to which they were built.

Industry and the Birmingham Canal Navigations have been in close partnership since the first coal boat made its way to Birmingham in 1769. Private capital invested in business was the mainstay of the industrial development that followed. Initially the Birmingham Canal Navigations built very few wharves and warehouses for the traders that used their waterway, but encouraged others to do so. Elsewhere, canal companies provided reasonable accommodation for their traders. Some were even palatial. These cathedral like structures rise several stories from the bank of the canal they once served.

It may be part of the Birmingham spirit, but people were willing to invest in new projects. Unhampered by the Guilds that existed in many other towns, they were to extend private enterprise to its fullest extent. The late Eric Foakes argued that Birmingham's growth through the canal age was constant and unhampered, seemingly, by the factors that affected trade in other towns such as Manchester; Birmingham, through diversity, was able to weather most storms. The canal, itself, was not a particular factor in this growth. Be that as it may, the Birmingham Canal promoted growth of industry by providing cheaper transport. Those engaged in the coal and iron industry found the canal a very useful tool.

The smelting of ironstone to make iron is just one of many processes to making finished iron articles. The people of Birmingham were adept at working metal into useful products, and had been engaged as such long before the Bridgewater and Sankey Canals were even thought of. Iron manufactured in charcoal furnaces, such as existed in Shropshire and more locally, at Aston, Cradley & Rushall, were enough to supply the manufacturers.

The establishment of iron smelting furnaces in the Black Country during the 1770s and 1780s accompanied the building of the first canals. With iron smelting came iron working, and the opportunity for expansion. Iron was now made by the coke smelting process. This method was able to produce iron in greater quantities. As blast furnace design was improved, the quantity of iron made increased. More and more blast furnaces also came into use, which led to an even greater production of iron. Several Birmingham businessmen, encouraged by the increasing supply, set up ironworks in the Black Country to

This building in Hall Street South was constructed in 1878 for offices and warehousing and to accommodate Kenrick's growing business, which had 700 employees.

Kenrick cast iron saucepan, late 19th century. The front is embossed "Kenrick" and '1¼ Gallon'.

Below Stairs of Hungerford Antiques

The Kenrick building in February 2016, with its distinctive spire.
Martin O'Keeffe

This crane was on a wharf adjacent to the Cape Hotel on Spon Lane; the Kenrick works spire (see photo left) is visible.
HNBC Weaver Collection

make cast iron hollowware. That is, pots and pans.

The first were Izon and Whitehurst, who established a foundry at Greet Mill beside the Birmingham Canal in 1782. They were followed in 1793 by Archibald Kenrick, who leased a piece of ground near Spon Lane to erect a new foundry. Kenrick had been a buckle maker in Birmingham, but had moved to West Bromwich to be near the foundry.

Kenrick's works were located near the old Birmingham Canal. Until 1790, the Spon Lane Locks had risen to a summit of 490 feet, but three locks had been removed, reducing the summit to 473 feet. The foundry was placed on the section formerly occupied by the upper locks, and was therefore on rising ground above the canal. The land owner was John Houghton, clerk to the BCN. In addition to Kenrick's works, there were a number of other lots.

Looking from Spon Lane Bridge, there was the 'Cape of Good Hope' public house, which had warehouses and wharves. Carriers' boats would call here to pick up and deliver goods for the neighbourhood. Later, Monk's packet boat stopped here on its journey between Tipton and Birmingham. The Spon Lane brassworks was next. Here, copper and calamine were mixed together to make brass. Houghton Street passed behind the brassworks and terminated near Kenrick's Foundry.

The original foundry was a small affair placed on the corner of Kenrick Street and Hall Street. In later years, it would be extended considerably occupying land to on the other side of Hall Street, which extended across the canal.

Hollowware manufacture requires iron and a lot of coal, both of which were readily obtainable by canal boat. The drawing depicts Kenrick's Foundry as it appeared about 1800. There is a small brick warehouse beside the canal, from where presumably cast hollowware was despatched.

The drawing is based on an early engraving which show the works and canalside. The crane, in the engraving, is shown to have a scale attachment which may have been used to weigh the pig iron.

There would have been cupolas, within the foundry, where the iron was melted down. Sand was an essential tool in the foundryman's art. A pattern of wood was used to form a shape within the sand, and it was into this shape that the molten metal was poured. Foundry sand was of a special quality and had to be dried. The ovens seen on the right of the picture may have used for that purpose. They are a different shape to the glede ovens normally associated with the coking of coal.

The bottle shaped oven, seen behind the warehouse, may not have been part of Kenrick's works, but one of the cones associated with the brassworks.

Kenrick's foundry grew in size and came to occupy a large piece of ground. A number of houses were built in nearby streets for the workers. The West Bromwich Tithe Map identifies the place as Kenrick's Village. By 1889, the foundry was on both sides of the canal. A narrow gauge railway was used to transport material within the works. This crossed the canal by a bridge.

Traffic records for May 1928 still show a busy canal trade. 110 tons of goods were taken to Turner's Wharf, beside the 'Cape of Good Hope', for shipment to Spon Lane Railway Basin. S Barlow brought 230 tons of coal from Pooley Hall Colliery, and George Hale 360 tons of coal from Tamworth Colliery. Another 55 tons came in C A Sadler's boats from Spon Lane railway basin. 94 tons of sand was brought by J Fletcher from sand quarries in the Stourbridge area. Rubbish and mud to local tips, moved in their own boats, accounted for another 290 tons. The coal traffic alone would have amounted to some 24 boats, and the rest perhaps another 18. This would equate to 9 or 10 boats a week.

Kenrick's Foundry is an enduring canal feature, despite being half hidden behind the piers of the elevated section of the M5 motorway. The distinctive offices serve as reminders of West Bromwich's rich industrial heritage. Although sadly, it is dwindling heritage, it is a credit to the builders that it has survived so long. It is unlikely that the same will be said of the motorway, whose crumbling piers already require heavy maintenance.

Late 19th century, small Kenrick cast iron flat iron, with a tubular steel handgrip.

Below Stairs of Hungerford Antiques

L is for Limestone Kiln

The drawing provides an illustration of the New Shaft kilns completed for the Earl of Dudley at Tipton, and which now feature as one of the attractions of the Black Country Living Museum.

Limestone was extracted for a number of reasons. The stone was burnt to make lime, an essential ingredient of mortar for building purposes, or as a fertiliser for the fields. It was also added as a flux in the iron smelting process, or crushed for road making. Limestone was taken by open work or by mining, and transported throughout the midlands by rail, road or canal.

The lime kiln was once a common canalside feature and was particularly found close to towns where stone brought by boat could be burnt to produce lime. The BCN was fortunately placed for limestone extraction. It was worked around Walsall, Darlaston and Dudley although not all locations were fortunate to be served by canal. Some quite lengthy tramroads were needed to transport the stone to the nearest canal wharf. It also varied in quality and quantity. Certain stones best suited the fertiliser trade, whilst others proved to be an excellent flux in the iron furnace.

Most West Midland lime kilns were small, and of the horseshoe type. That is they were built circular, but when viewed from above would resemble the shape of a horseshoe. Coal and limestone were bricked up in the kiln and left to burn for about a week, after which time the lime was removed and the kiln remade with a new charge. The continuous shaft kiln was more efficient. It was kept in use continually receiving the charge from above and producing lime at the bottom.

There had been shaft kilns near the Tipton portal of the Dudley Canal Tunnel, but these no longer survive. The New Kilns of 1842 remain almost intact and include a later extension, which is near the boat horse. The canal, beside it, known as the New Cut, was completed about 1839 and joined the old Birmingham Canal Main Line at Thomas Monk's boat dock. In fact, the making of the canal neatly bisected the old dock.

A 2ft 6in gauge tramway was laid above the kilns to bring limestone from mines such as East and West Castle. Another tramway ran down the left hand side to a crusher, where boats could be loaded with crushed stone.

In many parts where limestone abounds, it was often extracted as open work that is quarried. But around parts of Dudley and Walsall, miners tunnelled underground creating vast, and artificial, caverns underground. Working with tapers attached to their hats, or helmets, they worked with pick axes and gun powder to get the stone which was then raised to surface in the same fashion as coal, ironstone or fireclay.

This east side of Dudley abounded with limestone mines of various descriptions, and many of the limestone caverns still exist under the hillside. Those under Wrens Nest have been progressively filled in with sand to minimise any danger of collapse. Nearby, a labyrinth of subterranean canals can be visited, at least in part, by a ride on one the Dudley Canal Trust boats. These mines were able to supply limestone directly into boats. But there were many other places where the stone was raised by a conventional mine shaft to the surface and sent along a tramway to the boats.

The common craft employed to carry the stone or lime, was the typical BCN day boat and examples of such are shown in the drawing. Yet some lime masters had cabin boats for longer distance trade. George and H Strongitharm of Daw End had cabin boats which included *Safety*, *Star* and *Victoria* which were usually hauled by a pair of donkeys. Elias Crapper of the Hatherton Lime Works, Walsall had a pair of horse worked boats, *James* and *William*, which he used to carry lime.

Limestone and lime were also regular cargoes for some of the carrying firms. The Shropshire Union was noted for bringing stone from the quarries on its system, whilst Price and Co. made regular trips to Froghall and back for the Brierley Hill furnaces.

The biggest user of limestone in the Black Country was the iron smelting furnace. As this industry started to dwindle, so did the limestone trade. In later years the bulk of limestone was delivered to the surviving furnaces by rail wagon.

Virtually all types of BCN limestone traffic, all but cement, ceased during the 1920s. The last was to limekilns at Dudley Wood (J Flavel), Anchor Bridge, Oldbury (G Hale), and Waterfall Lane, Old Hill (Lowe Brothers) which was limestone collected from the GWR interchange basins at Oldbury or Wythymoor.

Limekilns are now a rarity in the West Midlands; most have been demolished, although there are good examples in other limestone districts. Those that deserve particular mention are Froghall (Caldon Canal), Llanymynech (Montgomery Canal) and Vroncysyllte (Llangollen Canal). Many are imposing structures, and rather larger than the New Kilns at Tipton.

This postcard shows the Lime Kilns around which the Black Country Living Museum is based. It was the inspiration for Edward's drawing.

M is for Mission

A growing concern was felt for the spiritual welfare of boatmen and their families during the nineteenth century, which led to a number of canal and dockside missions being built. The BCN had missions at Birmingham, Hednesford, Tipton, Walsall and Wolverhampton, which catered for the boating population.

The canal community, within the West Midlands, was a diverse group. Amongst their number were the day boatmen, the fly boatmen, those who worked 'family' boats, and the canal workers who maintained the waterways. Many lived on land and followed their religious beliefs as best as they could. The 'family' boat people spent most, or all, of their time afloat. It was a nomadic style of life of moving about the country from wharf to wharf. There was little time for religion or opportunity for education for the children. The boatman's missions remedied this problem by bringing religion and education to the workplace.

The first evidence of a mission to the local boat people was provided by voluntary organisations. The Inland Navigation Society, which had been set up by 1843, had a number of volunteers who went around the canal side at Tipton preaching to the boatmen there. They were followed by the Seamen and Boatmen's Friend Society which was established in 1846 to serve the needs of boatmen country-wide.

One of the first references to a boatmen's mission appears in the BCN Committee minutes for 1846. Shipton & Co asked for permission to moor a floating mission in the basin beside the Bilston Road in Wolverhampton. The application was declined, but it appears that a floating barge mission was established at Wolverhampton and maintained by the Bishop of Lichfield for a number of years. Later, in Birmingham, a canal-side mission room was established opposite the Top Lock of Farmer's Bridge locks, next to the Toll Office. This mission appears on maps from the 1850s, but little is known about its history or who was responsible for it.

The Incorporated Seamen and Boatmen's Friend Society had rented rooms, at Worcester Wharf, Birmingham, from about 1862, which were used as a Bethel Chapel. Attendances may not have been high, but things improved after Richard Cusworth was appointed Superintendent of the Birmingham Mission, in 1872. Cusworth, who had previously been involved with missionary work in India, replaced the Reverend James Pilkington at the Worcester Wharf Chapel. Richard Cusworth had both drive and ability, and it was through his efforts that a larger congregation was built up.

Worcester Wharf had been established by the Worcester & Birmingham Canal Company, but was now owned by the Sharpness New Docks & Gloucester & Birmingham Navigation Company. It comprised a mixture of carriers' depots, corn warehouses and timber yards. The Bethel Chapel was situated in their midst, beside the road which ran up on to Worcester Wharf from Wharf Street.

The continued survival of the Mission was threatened by new railway works planned by the Midland Railway Company. The land where the Bethel Chapel stood was needed for the new Central Goods Station. In March 1877, the IS & BFS applied to the SND&G&BNC for a new site on Worcester Wharf to build a Bethel School. The Canal Company asked their manager, W D George, to find out how many children might attend this school. George later reported that no more than 15 boat children would be of an age to attend the school. The SND&G&BNC decided that 'it would not be desirable to erect a school on Worcester Wharf' but agreed to investigate the matter of a site for reading rooms. The future of the Birmingham Mission was in doubt, but through a gift of £2000 from Miss Ryland, the Seamen and Boatmen's Friend Society were able to secure enough funds to build a new chapel on another part of the Worcester Wharf.

The new Boatmen's Mission Hall, designed by Osborn & Reading, was opened March 17th 1879. It was a tall three storied red brick building which straddled a narrow thoroughfare called the Gullet. On the ground floor were separate coffee rooms for the men and women, lavatories, a drying room and a kitchen where boatmen could cook their food. On the floor above was a lofty hall which could hold over 150 people, and above that were bedrooms for the caretaker.

A boat missionary's work could be a very demanding job. The holding of services was but a small part of the calling. The 'day' school at Worcester Wharf Mission for 1878 had an average daily attendance of 30 boat children, which was considerably higher than the figure Mr George had estimated the previous year. There was also a Sunday School which up 80 people would attend each week. The missionary would also go out to the community. Cusworth and his fellows at the Birmingham Mission had a wide area, which extended from Birmingham over much of the Black Country. Visits were made as far afield as Wolverhampton and Hednesford. During 1878, 7214 visits had been made to the cabins of boats and there were another 237 cases where missionaries had gone to see boatmen who lived ashore. There was also a small relief fund available from which they could make payments to boatmen in times of distress. Nearly 400 individual payments were made to local boatmen during the frost of 1878.

Unfortunately, the new Boatmen's Chapel had a brief existence. Birmingham Borough Council decided, in 1882, to make road improvements and extend Holliday Street through to Wharf Street by removing the Gullet and demolishing any buildings that stood in the path of the works. Miss Ryland's Committee looked for new premises. Negotiation went on with Birmingham Council, the Canal Company and the Midland Railway. In 1884 the Midland Railway provided a new site for the Mission which was at the corner of Bridge Street and Wharf Street. The Bridge Street Mission was completed by 1885. It was of similar design and had similar accommodation to the 1879 version. The Bridge Street Mission was opened in time for the Autumn meeting of the Seamen and Boatmen's Friend Society which was attended by delegates from all over the country. Special thanks were given to Miss Ryland for establishing the new Hall in Birmingham.

While the future of the Birmingham Boatmen's Mission was in doubt, a similar situation presented itself to the owners of the Wolverhampton Barge Mission. Their floating barge had gradually fallen into disrepair and the day school had to be closed. Church services were held, on a temporary basis, in the Shropshire Union Railway & Canal Company warehouse. During September 1882 the Reverend D R Norman, Rector of Stafford and secretary to the Lichfield Diocesan Barge Mission, asked the BCN for a piece of land, beside the top lock, Wolverhampton, to build a Mission Station Room. This was granted, and lease was to be prepared for a nominal annual rent of £1. Plans were drawn up, in due course, for the building by a Mr Fleming, architect, which were passed to the BCN committee for approval at their December 1883 meeting. A formal lease was then drawn up and the mission room was erected during 1884.

The drawing shows boats moored alongside the Mission and School at Hednesford. This building was completed in 1885 on a strip of land beside the canal, for the Incorporated Seamen and Boatmen's Friend Society. The site, which lay on the offside of the canal between the Railway Bridge and Hemlocks Bridge, had been given to the Society by Messrs Williams.

The first the BCN committee knew about this was detailed in a letter which was read out during their monthly meeting on August 29th, 1884. The Seamen and Boatmen's Friend Society wrote to request permission to make an entrance from their property on to the canalside, and also for a contribution towards the cost of construction. It was estimated that £400 was needed to complete the building and £320 had already been collected by their committee. The BCN decided, at a subsequent meeting, to levy a charge of one shilling per year for the use of the entrance on to their property, but regretted that they could not make a contribution towards the cost. The BCN committee did later make one concession. During the February 1885 meeting, it was agreed to send out a circular for contributions for the Hednesford Mission with the dividend warrants, and this enabled individual BCN staff to make a donation towards the cause.

Hednesford Mission was formerly opened on 26 June 1885 by Sir Richard Moon. A report describing the events was published the next day in the Birmingham Daily Post:

A Boatman's Mission Hall and Coffee Room has been erected on land near the Hednesford Canal Wharf, by the Birmingham Centre of the Seamen's & Boatmen's Friend Society, of which Mr W.W Pilcher is chairman. The building consists of a mission hall, which will seat about 120 persons; a coffee room and reading room, separated from the mission room by a movable screen; and a residence for a local missionary; and has been built by Mr T Mason of Hednesford, under the direction of Mr A.T Greening, architect, Birmingham. The General Committee have appointed Mr P Worrall as missionary, and he will not only have charge of the mission, but will also visit the various canal wharves in the Cannock district, and also the canals as far as Walsall and Wolverhampton. The hall was opened yesterday by Mr Moon, chairman of the London and North Western Railway Company. Among those present were the Rev Canon Wilkinson, Rev R.W Cusworth, Captain Douglas Galton, C.B., Mr Brydore, government inspector of canal boats, Mr W.W Pilcher, Mr Evans (Kenilworth),. Mr Southall (Birmingham), Mr J. Schofield, treasurer of the S and B.F. Society, &c. - Mr Pilcher read a report, which showed that the entire cost of the building and furniture would be about £600., towards which £310. was raised by a bazaar in Birmingham. The proprietors, officials and servants of the Birmingham Canal contributed £216., Miss Ryland £105., per Mr Postans £31.,and general public £136., which enabled the committee to pay all expenses and open the mission free of debt. - Mr Moon, in opening the hall said the building was erected for the welfare of those who lived on our canals, and they were finishing material work in connection with the place, and commencing the spiritual work. He trusted that the understanding would prove a blessing to the body, the minds, and the spirits of those for whom it was intended, - Canon Wilkinson, in addressing the meeting, spoke of his experience with the Mission Hall at Worcester Wharf, Birmingham, and trusted the one they were opening would also be successful. Addresses were also given by Mr W Evans and Mr J Schofield, and the proceedings terminated with a hearty vote of thanks to Mr Moon for attending.

The location of missions was carefully thought out. They were always situated at places where boats gathered, and frequently these gatherings were of an enforced nature. Boats could be held up waiting for loads or passage. At Hednesford, the reason for the delay involved the wait for a load of coal. Some boats could be tied up for a day before they were loaded. The mission

Boatmen's Hall, Hednesford.

Hednesford. Coal from East Cannock, West Cannock, Cannock and Rugeley and the Cannock Chase Collieries (No 9 and 10 pits) was loaded into boats here. A number of empty and loaded day boats fill the canal from side to side. One or two long distance boats can be seen too. A coal train is crossing the canal on the London & North Western Railway, which, despite being in competition with canals, had controlled the BCN since 1845. Hednesford Mission is on the right.

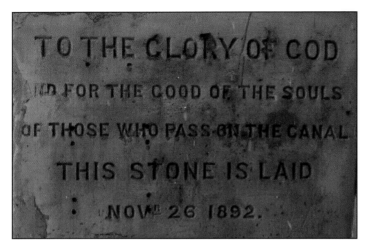

Dedication stone, Tipton Mission.

Tipton Mission, 1968.
Keith Hodgkins

provided a place for the boat people to go. The coffee and reading rooms were an alternative to the public house. Here too was the opportunity for the boat children to learn to read and write whilst their parents' boat awaited its turn at the loading wharf.

At Worcester Wharf and Gas Street Basin, there were similar gatherings of boats waiting their turn for the wharves and warehouses. The Bridge Street Mission was ideally placed to serve both. The day school in Bridge Street was run by a Miss Hutchings who taught the basics of reading, writing and arithmetic. For many boat children this was the only education they got. Missions such as Bridge Street continued to provide a base for preaching to the boat people where the Mission Superintendent and lay preachers would go out to the local boat communities. In addition to the cabin visits, sometimes open air services would be held. The following is reproduced from the Waterman (December 1913) which recalls the 1890s when E Clark, the writer, was a missionary there:

The Worcester Wharf, the Bar Lock, Shropshire Union, and Fazeley Street, and other wharves, made excellent centres for open air preaching. Our Method was this: we visited a wharf on a summer's evening, or on a Sunday morning, and found, perhaps, from 12 to 20 canal boats "tied up," lying together, containing a population of from 40 to 50 men and women, besides a number of children. We decided that this was the spot and time for a service. So returning to the adjacent Hall we gathered together several helpers, and brought out the little portable harmonium and a quantity of hymn books (Sankey's) and proceeded at once to the Wharf. Mounting the quay-side we gave out the hymn book to the "congregation" - some standing on their "hatches" others sitting on the sides of their boats while the children were grouped about us. The Missionary stepped on to the top of a cabin, which was his "pulpit" and gave on a hymn.

Tipton also benefited from a boatmen's mission erected beside the Top Lock, at Factory, between 1892 and 1893. This mission, like Wolverhampton, was run by the Lichfield Diocesan Barge Mission. Mrs Legge, wife of the Bishop of Lichfield, had the honour of laying the foundation stone for the Mission when work began in November 1892. This Mission, like all its counterparts located elsewhere, served the needs of the boatmen. Tipton Top Lock was a busy place for boats. Not only did boats wait their turn for the locks, but they also were tied up waiting orders. For here was the place boats of William & Samuel Foster congregated when they were not working loads to Ellesmere Port, London or Manchester.

The Tipton Boat Mission still survives today, although in an altered form. For the keen eyed it is still possible to find the foundation stone and read the inscription:

TO THE GLORY OF GOD...FOR THE GOOD OF THE SOULS OF THOSE WHO PASS ON THE CANAL THIS STONE IS LAID NOVEMBER 26th 1892.

A third mission was completed for the Incorporated Seamen & Boatmen's Friend Society in 1901 at the Top Lock Walsall. Unlike the other two missions owned by the Society, this was designated a 'Boatman's Rest' to cater for the boatmen waiting their turn for the locks. The laying of the foundation stone was mentioned in the Birmingham Weekly Post, 22 September 1900:

On Tuesday, the foundation stone was laid of a Boatman's Rest, on the side of the Birmingham Canal, Birchills Locks, Walsall, under the auspices of the Incorporated Seamen's and Boatmen's Friend Society. Mr A Arter, of London (chairman of the society), presided over a large gathering, which included the town clerk (Mr J.R Cooper), Messrs Joel Cadbury (Chairman of the Midland Committee). A.J Smith (Bristol), Captain Simpson (Liverpool), Captain Hewitt, Messr G.J Blunn, G.R Jebb, W Evans (Birmingham). Revds R.W Cusworth (Superintendent of the Society's Works), J.W Cannings (organising secretary), L.W Parry, F.W Brown (Bristol), J.F Buckler (Plymouth,) E Clark (London) and S Bentham (Liverpool). The building is to comprise a coffee and reading room and a mission room, and the cost will be £350 - Mr Cadbury explained that the rest was to form a new centre of mission work in connection with the society. The Birmingham Canal Company had 100 (sic) miles of canals, and conveyed about eight million tons of goods annually. As regards the Walsall district, the number of boats passing through the Birchills Locks averaged 160 per day in summer, and in winter 200. Consequently there was frequently a great congestion of traffic, and boatmen had often to wait two or three hours to get their boats through. The Birmingham missionaries who had visited the neighbourhood during the last fifteen years had been very much impressed by the need of accommodation of the kind it was now proposed to provide. The Birmingham Canal Company had given the site. In due course it was hoped to appoint a missionary to the new centre.- The Mayor of Walsall laid the foundation stone, and expressed his warm sympathy with the objects of the society and his appreciation of the boon with which the building would confer upon the class for whose benefit it was intended. He believed it was only necessary for the work of the society to become known in Walsall for the debt on the building to be entirely wiped off. (Hear, Hear,) - Mr T Jones (Bushbury) laid a second stone - Those present were afterwards entertained to luncheon by the Mayor.

The Walsall Mission is now the only BCN mission building which survives intact. Sadly the foundation stone is badly weathered, but it is still possible to read most of the names inscribed. The building was for several years the home of the Birchills Canal Museum and was open to the public at certain times. Sadly this has now closed, although the building still survives unaltered beside the top lock.

Lock Cottage and former Mission (later canal museum, since closed), Birchills, Walsall, 1996.   *Brenda Ward*

N is for Nine Locks

Although it is common for canal bridges, junctions, locks and tunnels to be named after existing places in the locality, sometimes the reverse happens and a canal side feature lends its name to the area where it is located. Such is the case with Nine Locks, Brierley Hill. When first completed, the nine locks, which took the canal up to the 'Level' would have been considered an important local feature. As industry and housing was developed around them, a colliery, ironworks and a limekiln all adopted the name Nine Locks. There is every reason to suppose that houses and cottages near the lock flight were also known as Nine Locks.

The general area is known as the Delph, or Black Delph, and it is by this latter name that the lock flight is better known. Delph Locks are situated at one extremity of the Birmingham Canal Navigations. Beyond them lies the Stourbridge Canal, which, in turn, joins the Staffordshire and Worcestershire Canal at Stewponey. The Birmingham and Stourbridge canals are part of a number of interconnected waterways that cross Central England. This important transport network grew from canals such as these, and contributed to the development of commerce and industry during the eighteenth and nineteenth centuries.

The local glass and iron industry provided the incentive for the construction of the canals in this area. Rich deposits of coal and ironstone were eagerly sought after. Two canal companies, the Dudley and the Stourbridge, were formed to exploit the district. The Stourbridge Canal from Stewponey to the Delph was completed in December 1779. The Dudley, which joined the Stourbridge at the Delph, was, at first, only two and a quarter miles long. It climbed immediately by nine locks to the Ox Leasowes, where the original terminus was located.

The Stourbridge was well supplied with water; the Grove, Middle and Fens Pools provided more than enough water for navigation. The Dudley was far less fortunate. A small reservoir at Woodside was supplemented by water from local mines.

When the Nine Locks were completed in June 1779, long side pounds were provided for each lock. The locks were not evenly spaced; No's 3 and 4 formed a pair where boats immediately went from one to the other. No's 5, 6 and 7 were also arranged together in a similar fashion to that which is found at the Bratch Locks (Staffs & Worcester Canal). This must have impeded navigation as only one boat could pass either group at a time.

This was a design feature common with works engineered by Thomas Dadford and his sons. Dadford made this arrangement on locks 9 & 10 on the Stourbridge Canal, where he was engineer. He continued this practice at the Delph where height was required in a relatively short distance. Bratch had been a conventional Brindley staircase set of three locks, but Dadford changed this arrangement to reduce the loss of water through the flight. Similar arrangements were to be found on the Montgomeryshire and Glamorgan canals.

After the Stourbridge Canal was finished in 1779, trade was able to flow along both waterways. Coal mines at the Level and Woodside benefited immediately. Business entrepreneurs Richard and William Croft were quick to realise the possibilities of local iron manufacture. By 1786 they had erected a furnace on the Level Colliery.

The Dudley Canal proprietors were keen to extend their waterway to join the Birmingham Canal at Tipton. This was accomplished in 1792 with the completion of the 3154 yard long Dudley Tunnel. A more ambitious scheme resulted in a further extension to Selly Oak in 1798 through the 3795 yard long Lapal Tunnel. Reservoirs at Gads Green, and later Lodge Farm, were able to provide an improved water supply.

The links to three other canals did much to improve trade on the Dudley Canal, particularly in coal, ironstone and iron goods. Carriers commenced to use the waterway, bringing merchandise to Stourbridge, or passing onto the Staffordshire and Worcestershire Canal. Trade for and from the River Severn often passed this way in preference to Wolverhampton. J G Ames, George Ryder Bird and Crowley & Company were all regular carriers on the Dudley and Stourbridge Canals. Local canal carriers were William Price & Son of Brierley Hill and William Mullet of Rock Hill.

At the top of Nine Locks were the Nine Locks and Brierley Hill Ironworks. They stood on either side of Mill Street. George and Thomas Holcroft had started the first Nine Locks Ironworks standing on the west side of Mill Street about 1800. The ironworks was later taken over by the Hornblower family who also converted the Flour Mill on the east side of Mill Street into an ironworks. This became the Brierley Hill Ironworks. A steel plant was constructed on this site, similar to that which then existed at the Brades, Oldbury.

The Cementation Process manufactured steel at this time. The tall conical brick furnaces produced blister steel, which was refined in clay crucibles. The Hornblowers were bankrupt in 1824 and the British Iron Company purchased the works. Brierley Hill Ironworks then became known as Nine Locks Ironworks and continued to produce finished iron. The steel making plant was transferred to Corngreaves.

Other industry was developing in the area. On the Stourbridge Canal near Black Delph Junction, a Fire Brick Factory was established which sent most of its produce by canal. Fireclay is a greyish stone, which is mined in the same way as coal, and frequently the measure of fireclay lies close to the coal seams. Fireclay was noted for its heat resisting properties and it was used to make bricks, gas retorts and glasshouse pots. Fireclay was only raised in certain parts of the Black Country. One of the largest and most successful districts lay between Wordsley and the Delph. With the rapid rise of the local iron industry during the nineteenth century, there was a large demand for firebricks particularly for the lining of furnaces.

The Dudley Canal was constantly affected by mining subsidence, and maintenance took a severe toll on company profits. On 27 June 1846, the Dudley Canal amalgamated with the Birmingham Canal Navigations and thereafter Paradise Street

A view looking up seven of the Delph locks from the bottom lock, No. 8.

Offices controlled the affairs of the canal.

The BCN made many improvements. Lines of canal were straightened and bridges were replaced. The biggest scheme happened between 1856 and 1858 when Netherton Tunnel and the Two Lock line were completed. New locks also replaced the old Delph Locks, in part. The first and ninth were retained, but the rest were abandoned after a new flight of six locks was constructed along a shorter course in 1858. They were deeper and their route was cut across the side ponds of the old flight. Delph nine rise now became Delph eight rise.

Although the old locks fell into disuse, the lock house and nearby canal cottage remained, and can still be seen near the old line. Another toll house was constructed close to the 'new' No. 4 lock. A portion of the old line stayed in water. The piece from the pound between (old) No. 1 and (new) No. 2 served limekilns and a sawmill.

There was an important colliery near the Nine Locks Ironworks, which was worked by the Earl of Dudley. This pit was the scene of a serious pit disaster on Wednesday 17 March 1869. Thirteen miners and six horses were imprisoned in the mine after water flooded in. A remarkable rescue attempt was rapidly launched, where many in the locality gave a hand. All but one was saved in consequence. The most remarkable being the saving of Benjamin Higgs who survived 140 hours underground. Opposite Nine Locks Ironworks was Nine Locks Basin that served as a boatage depot for the Shropshire Union Company. This depot was completed in 1889 and was open by the end of May. Railway boats from this and other local depots plied through Netherton Tunnel to the various Railway Interchange Basins on the other side. Next to this basin was the BCN public wharf, which was also known as Nine Locks Wharf. The first lock was above Mill Street Bridge, which was also known as Nine Locks Bridge. In later years there was a toll house here, which had replaced the house near No. 4 lock.

The stable block placed beside the present No. 3 lock is survivor from the age when horses provided the haulage for most canal craft. Once, canal side stables were common, particularly in the Black Country where the commonest canal craft was the horse drawn day boat. Edward Paget Tomlinson's drawing shows the view by the third lock looking towards the bottom lock at the Delph. The tall chimneys belonged to Pearson's Firebrick works, which provided the last fireclay boatage traffic on this canal. The loaded boat in the lock is carrying minerals, which could have been coal, ironstone or fireclay. The stables are shown to the left of the lock. They date from the late nineteenth century and still retain the old wooden stalls inside the building. There were also other stables in the area, which were used by the boat horses. One is known to have been in Mill Street near the Nine Locks Ironworks.

Mining subsidence affected both the old and new locks at the Delph, and BCN labourers found regular employment there maintaining their structure. Evidence of their work is visible today particularly at the second lock where the original lock chamber has been virtually buried beneath newer brickwork above.

Further down the locks, there were no underlying coal seams, and the chambers remain in the form they were built. Delph Road crosses the entrance to Delph Bottom Lock. Above the lock the canal widens out and provided moorings for boats, which first served as the BCN Black Delph Wharf.

Change is ever present in the modern West Midland Canal network. Much of the trappings of industry have been swept away and replaced by residential and retail properties. The winter of 1997-98 saw heavy contractors plant move in to a site above the top lock at the Delph. The canal was closed between Level Street Bridge and Mill Street. Contractors set to work cutting a new and straighter canal through the hillside and filling in the part that curved round by the Merry Hill Shopping Centre. At this point the canal is far above the Centre on a high embankment.

By Easter 1998 the new waterway was reopened for canal navigation, but the towpath remained closed for a few more months. Most of the new canal is a concrete lined trough, wide and deep, unlike the old weed-clogged canal.

Delph Locks are part of the cruising route from Birmingham through to the Staffordshire & Worcestershire Canal and the River Severn, and are quite busy in the summer months. They are a pleasant walk and are kept tidy by the Canal & River Trust. It is also possible to trace the course of the old line of locks, which were filled in after the new line opened. One, near the stable block, has been excavated and rebuilt as a feature. Thus the traces of the past are still to be found, but it takes a little time to search them out.

The bottom of the Delph flight in 1971; the western point of the BCN, showing coalfields and factories.   *Bob May Collection*

A fairly recent view of Nine Locks, Delph.
Brenda Ward

The same locks, from a similar position, but several decades before,
showing the boat horse stables.

O is for Ocker Hill

If the Birmingham Canal Navigations are acknowledged to be at the centre of the canal network, then Tipton must be considered to lie at their heart. There was nowhere else on the BCN where canals were so concentrated. Wherever one would walk, it was difficult not to avoid seeing or passing a canal. Ocker Hill is situated along the north-east corner of the parish, near Leabrook and the boundary with the neighbouring parish of Wednesbury.

Ocker Hill had rich seams of coal, which were exploited during the late part of the eighteenth and early part of the nineteenth century. The Moat Colliery Company had a number of shafts in the area. Some mine shafts were close to the canal, with the workings passing under the waterway at several intervals.

In later years, this area was to be badly affected by subsidence and the land dropped considerably in relation to the canal. The BCN fought a constant battle to keep the level, and protect the canal banks. The canal company added so much earth and spoil, that the line of the waterway eventually stood on an embankment. Houses and other buildings formerly on a level with the canal were now considerably below it.

A branch canal (473 feet level) to Ocker Hill had been part of the original BCN canal act, but the line of route was altered prior to construction. The Ocker Hill branch, completed by 1774, ran from the Old Birmingham Canal to the terminus beside the turnpike road from Wolverhampton to Birmingham at Ocker Hill (some maps call it Ochre Hill). Here a wharf was laid out, and a group of canal-side cottages erected.

The building of the Broadwaters Extension Canal (later part of the Walsall Canal) for the Birmingham & Fazeley Canal Company created a need to recirculate water back to the summit level. Water would otherwise be irretrievably lost as every boat went up or down to the mines on that part of the canal.

It was decided to erect a pumping engine at the end of the Ocker Hill branch, which was the spot closest to both levels. A cut was made from the 408 ft level through to Ocker Hill. Part of this cut passed through the hillside in a brick lined tunnel, until it reached the place below where the engine was intended to be situated. The decision was made before the Birmingham and Fazeley Act was approved. An engine (or proposed engine) to 'return the water' is shown on John Snape's 1783 survey for the intended waterway. At this time, the BCN and B & F were independent concerns, but even at the planning stage, provision had to be made to safeguard the water lost from the Birmingham Canal.

When work started on the Birmingham-Fazeley Canal from Ryder's Green down to the 408 feet level at Broadwaters, the two canal companies had merged into one concern, the Birmingham & Birmingham & Fazeley Canal. Work went ahead to build the new canal during 1785 and 1786. When the first boats started to use this waterway, the need for pumping water back to the higher level would have been paramount.

It seems the engine was in place before the Broadwaters Extension was finished. An order was placed with Boulton and Watt by the 'old' Birmingham Canal Company at the end of 1783, and it appears that the engine was erected in 1784. In those days, many of the parts were supplied by other ironmasters such as John Wilkinson. Both this and the second engine, supplied in 1791, were made in this fashion. The cylinder for the 1791 engine was cast at Bersham, and taken by road to Ocker Hill where it was left in the field near to the place where it was to be erected.

The location of the pumping plant at Ocker Hill became immensely important to the BCN during the nineteenth century as trade on the waterway improved, and the canal system was extended. The number of pumping engines was increased. There were four at work by 1825, and by 1900, six were needed.

Philip Weaver compiled the following list for the Railway & Canal Historical Society Journal in 1986, which provides useful information concerning the steam pumping engines, and is worth reproduction:

Early engines, which are known to have been erected at Ocker Hill are as follows;
1784 Boulton and Watt 46 in x 8ft, 24 in pump lifting 66 ft 45 ihp, 1791 Boulton and Watt 46 in x 8ft, 24 in pump lifting 66 ft 45 ihp, 1803 Boulton and Watt 46 in x 8ft, 24 in pump lifting 66 ft, 1825 Boulton and Watt 46 in x 8ft, 24 in pump lifting 66 ft.
Of these, the 1803 engine was first supplied to the BCN with an iron beam and parallel motion, while the 1825 one was originally supplied in 1811 and first used at Caponfield. The plant as it existed in 1902 comprised the following engines, all installed in a common house:
tJo.l Compound beam engine purchased new from Coalbrookdale Company in 1883, started work 29 June 1883
Cylinders: 17K in and 31K in x 7ft 6in stroke: 129 ihp

Pumps: one 28% in plunger and one 35Km bucket

Output: at 905 strokes per minute, 175 locks per day.

No 2 Single-acting Cornish engine, purchased second hand from Gilpin & Co, Pelsall in 1866 whose origin and maker were unknown.

Cylinder. 62K in bore x 8ft stroke. 63 ihp at 12 strokes per minute

Pump: one 38 in bucket lift

Output at 9.5 strokes per minute, 215 locks per day

No 3 Single-acting beam type by Boulton & Watt in 1837

Cylinder: 46% in bore x 7ft 6in stroke, 63ihp at 12 strokes per minute.

Pump: one 24 in bucket lift

Output at 12 strokes per minute, 103 locks per day.

No A Compound beam engine recorded at Coalbrookdale Company in 1883, but possibly a rebuild by them of an earlier engine as cost was only £1,475 compared with £2,320 for No 1. Started work 17th May 1884. Details are the same as for the No.1 engine.

No 5 Single-acting beam type built by James Watt & Co in 1851.

Cylinder: 48K in bore x 7ft 9in stroke.150 ihp at 10 strokes per minute

Pump: one 32 in bucket lift

Output at 10 strokes per minute, 154 locks per day

No 6 Double-acting beam type by G BrJ

Davis,date and origin unknown. Purchased second hand in 1857 as standby. Was originally a "forge engine", presumably a furnace blowing engine, and converted by BCN. Being double acting, it operated two pump-lifts, one plunger, and one bucket.

Cylinder: 48 in bore x 7ft 6in stroke. 227 ihp at 8 strokes per minute.

Pumps: one 32 in bucket lift, one 32 in plunger lift

Output at 8 strokes per minute, 240 locks per day

The collective horsepower of the engines was 906, and the plant was capable of lifting 1,062 locks in twenty four hours, approximately 26.5 million gallons. The lift was 66 feet. It is worth noting that all six engines were installed side-by-side in the same building, making it one of the largest, if not the largest, indoor installation of beam engines in the country - a distinction often claimed for the allegedly unique six-engine house on Severn Tunnel.

In 1897 the original Boulton & Watt engine from Smethwick (1779) was removed to Ocker Hill for preservation, being steamed on the occasion of the Watt Centenary, in 1919 and possibly other occasions.

No details have survived of the boilers used prior to 1904, but it is known that the two Coalbrookdale compounds worked at 70 pounds per square inch and the other four engines at 25 psig. It is presumed that the new, separate boilers were installed for the compounds in 1883-4.

The new plant installed in 1903-4 consisted of three engines as described below plus the old No. 6 engine, the latter being kept as a standby and supplied with steam from the main boilers through a reducing valve at 25 psig.

Engines: Vertical, triple-expansion, three-throw type built by Hathorn Davey, Leeds, in 1904.

Cylinder: High pressure 13in bore x 3ft stroke, intermediate pressure 21 in bore x 3ft stroke

Low-pressure 34in bore x 3ft stroke

Normal running speed: 29 revolutions per minute.

Pumps: Three direct-coupled plunger pumps per engine, 23 in bore x 3 ft stroke.

Output: Combined delivery from three engines, 808 locks per day. Maximum delivery of plant, 1048 locks per day or 26.2 million gallons raised 66 feet.

Two views at Ocker Hill.

Ocker Hill - power station.
Bob May Collection

At the bottom of Ryders Green Locks, with Ocker Hill power station in the distance, the photographer is standing on the towpath bridge across the Haines branch. This is followed by the entrance to the Midland Railway Great Bridge basin. On the right is L&NWR Great Bridge basin. Note the steam locomotives lined up on the railway bridge, probably awaiting scrapping.
Weaver Collection

P is for Packet Boat

Various canal carriers operated packet boats on local waterways. From 1798, packet boats were tried on the Birmingham Canal Navigations, The Dudley No.2 Canal, Warwick & Birmingham and the Worcester & Birmingham. All, of these, evidently did not last long.

The Worcester & Birmingham Packet was tried from Hopwood to Worcester Wharf in Birmingham, whilst the Dudley Canal packet ran from Netherton to Worcester Wharf. The Netherton Boat was perhaps the most ambitious of the lot, commencing service after the opening of the Lapal Tunnel; it was routed through the two-mile long tunnel and timed to reach Birmingham in five hours!

All packet boats carried both passengers and parcels. There were selected points where the boats would call to set down and pick up passengers, and they operated to an advertised timetable. Fares were charged according to distance, and two different classes of travel were provided: first and second-class.

On the Birmingham Canal, traffic was handled in the hold of the day boat or the carrier's flyboat. And, although the BCN concentrated on the carriage of freight, there were occasions where Packet Boats have operated. These vessels had sleeker hulls and were pulled at speed, often by a team of horses. A Birmingham trade directory for 1801 stated that a packet boat operated from

The scene in the drawing. Galton Bridge - without the packet boat, but with a L&NWR engine and passenger train on the Stour Valley line. The building of it beside the canal is mentioned in the *S is for Steward Aqueduct* chapter.

Friday Bridge to Tipton. There is no mention of who operated it, but it seems to have only been of short duration. Similar packets were also tried along the Worcester & Birmingham Canal from Birmingham to Hopwood and Netherton. Neither lasted any significant time.

The Euphrates Packet

Thomas Monk commenced another packet from Friday Bridge, Birmingham to Factory Bridge, and Tipton during the early 1820s. Monk was a Tipton Green boat-builder, who operated the boat on three days a week: Monday, Thursdays and Saturdays. His *Euphrates Packet* left Mr Joseph Aston's: Factory Bridge at 8.15 a.m. and completed the journey to Birmingham in two hours. The route was via the 'Old Main Line' passing through Dudley Port, Tividale, Oldbury, Spon Lane, Smethwick and Winston Green before finishing the journey near Friday Bridge. It returned at 5 p.m. from Birmingham. The price from Tipton was 1s 6d First Class Cabin and 1s in the Second Class cabin.

In June 1830, Thomas Monk started his boat from Wolverhampton leaving Mr Shipton's Wharf at 6 a.m. and travelling by the way of Deepfields, the Fox Inn near Wednesbury Oak, and Bloomfield, before picking up the original route from Factory. The journey time to Birmingham is not stated but was

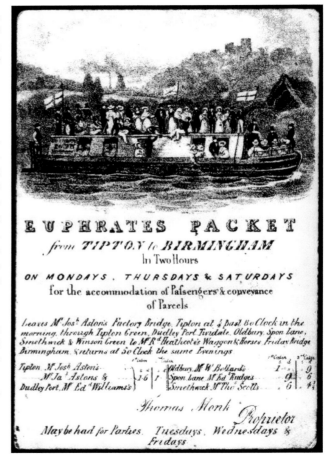

Advertising card for Thomas Monk fly boat c 1820.
Bob May Collection

likely to be over four hours. The return boat left Birmingham, as before, at 5 p.m. By now the service frequency had risen to six days a week (Monday-Saturday). The fare from Wolverhampton to Birmingham was 2s 6d First Class, 1s 9d Second Class.

Further alterations to Monk's packet schedule happed when the New Main Line was nearing completion. A notice for October 1837 stated the intention of the Euphrates Packet Company to commence running their packet from Deepfields to Birmingham in two and half hours. The service was to run Mondays, Tuesdays, Thursdays, Fridays and Saturdays, starting at Mr Richard Thompson's Boat Inn, Deepfields at 8 a.m. On the Wednesday, the Packet left James Aston's Fountain Inn, Tipton, at 8.30 a.m. for Wolverhampton.

In 1843 Monk's packet was replaced by a faster service, which followed the new line of the canal. These boats were operated by the Swift Packet Company, which had James Shipton as a managing partner. They ran boats between Wolverhampton and Birmingham. A team of three horses were employed and these were changed at regular intervals.

The Swift Packet

Swift Packet Company ran the Packet boat, which was a partnership of members of the firm of James Shipton and Co. They purchased boats made in Scotland, and used a type of boat developed by William Houston, one of the proprietors of the Glasgow, Paisley and Johnstone canal, which were 70ft long and 6ft wide.

The service commenced on 1 August 1843 and ran daily, Sundays excepted, until early 1852. It ceased when the trains started to run between Birmingham and Wolverhampton.

Initially, two boats ran each way. At the peak of service, in 1846, seven boats made the journey between the two towns. Later, six boats a day was the usual timetable. It ran from Railway Street near the Canal Bridge (later Broad Street Bridge) in Wolverhampton to the Packet Wharf, Great Charles Street, and Birmingham.

There was a two-tier fare structure: chief cabin and second cabin. Fares were priced from Wolverhampton to Birmingham and vice versa; fares for total distance 1s 6d (chief cabin) and 1s (second). Cheaper fares were available for shorter distances.

By 1846 the second cabin fare had risen to 1s 2d.

Although advertised in the Wolverhampton Chronicle from the start, Birmingham papers do not seem to mention it until much later. The Birmingham Journal for 27 April 1844, has an entry that refers to three boats travelling each way; by 11 May, 1844, this service had increased to four, with omnibus connections quoted for Dudley. There was also an additional short working between Birmingham & Tipton. People wishing to visit the Dudley Castle grounds were advised to secure their places at least a day in advance for the 9 or 11 o'clock departures from Birmingham.

The Swift Packet paid a fixed annual toll for the use of the canal. By 1845 this was set at £800. In response from the Iron and Coal masters in 1845, the Swift Packet Co. was given preference over all others at locks, which improved their time-keeping. However the speed of the boats did not leave the banks undamaged. In 1847 James Shipton appeared before the BCN committee to explain the great injury done to the canal works. Extra payment was sought and the annual toll was increased to £1000. By November 1850, Shipton and Company were requesting a reduction on this annual payment, no doubt in view of the impending threat from railway competition. The committee chose not to agree to any reduction.

The omnibus connection ran from Tipton Factory to Wright's offices in Dudley High Street.

Several boats were used on this service. The timetable was such that boats left Birmingham and Wolverhampton at similar times; at least four boats must have been in service at any one time. The fleet therefore must have been greater, perhaps five or six, to allow for craft under repair.

All boats seem to have been named, and they include the *Arrow* and the *Victory*. They had a long passenger cabin, and sawdust was used to cover the floor. All manner of people travelled by the Swift Packet, but no one was safe from pickpockets. In January 1846 a clerk, employed at the London Works at Smethwick, travelled on the packet to Wolverhampton. He boarded the *Arrow* at Monument Lane Bridge and paid his fare when the boat reached Summit Bridge. At Wolverhampton, the man discovered that his wallet had gone. All he could remember was that a suspicious looking character had sat next to him dressed as a sailor.

The right that gave Packet Boats preference at the locks became part of the BCN Bye-Laws in March 1845. Several prosecutions were made from November 1845 onwards, where those that delayed the boat were fined 40 shillings. It annoyed other boatmen intensely. Often, seeing the packet coming, they would make haste to get into the locks first. On 23 January 1846, the *Victory* was approaching Tipton locks. William Stevenson was the captain. A boatman, Thomas Cresswell, deliberately got his boat into the path of the packet and stubbornly refused to give way. Stevenson and others on the packet tried to pull Creswell's boat back. But Thomas coiled his rope around the paddle start and threatened to ram the packet boat. The *Victory* was seriously delayed that day.

The Swift Packet operated from the top of Great Charles Street near Friday Bridge. Here there was a number of canal side wharves and warehouses beside the Newhall Branch. The Packet Station was reached from the access road near 153 and 154 Great Charles Street. Here, Shipton and Company also had warehouses and wharves for their carrying business. In 1847 the carrying business was taken over by the North Staffordshire Railway, but the Packet Boat continued to start here. The Packet normally completed the journey in two hours and provided a useful service. It continued to run until December 1851 when water shortages rather than the impending opening of the Stour Valley Railway were given as the reason for the curtailment of the service:

Notice to the Public
Swift Packets

In consequence of the short supply of water in the Birmingham Canal the Proprietor of the above Packets are reluctantly compelled to DISCONTINUE them. In doing so they beg to tender their thanks for the very liberal patronage bestowed upon them during the last eight years.

For a very considerable time they have had to trespass upon the patience of passengers travelling by them; and now that they are thrown out of time almost every journey, they prefer giving them up altogether rather than continue to break faith with the public, which they regret to say they have been compelled to do.
N.B - They will be discontinued at the end of the present week.

Wolverhampton, Tuesday, December 2 1851.

(As reproduced from the Wolverhampton Chronicle December 3rd 1851)

Passenger traffic on the Stour Valley Railway did not start until July 1852, yet despite this fact, the packet boats were disposed of and the Swift Packet Company ran no further boat service. Some of the craft were to enjoy a further period of existence. Three of the boats were sold to the Shropshire Union Canal Company in February 1852 who wished to start a new packet boat on the Montgomeryshire Canal from Newtown to Rednal. Here the boats met a morning train from Birkenhead, Chester and Shrewsbury at Rednal and passengers transferred to the Packet that had arrived from Newtown. Calling points were Welshpool and Newtown with a journey of about 5 hours that passed 22 locks. This service was referred as the Swift Passenger, a second service was offered from Llangollen Road Station (beside the towpath south end Whitehouse Tunnel) to Llangollen, known as Quick Passenger Boats. This second service operated three boats each way and crossed the Pontcysyllte Aqueduct to reach Llangollen.

<u>William Bishton's Packet Boat</u>

A third packet boat operated through Netherton Tunnel. In 1858, Mr Bishton of Wolverhampton approached the BCN to run a packet three times a day between Netherton and Dudley Port Stations. This service started running the next year between Bishton's Bridge at Netherton and Dudley Port Railway Station, where connections were made with the various railway services to Birmingham, Wolverhampton and Walsall. The period of operation is uncertain, but did not extend for many years.

<u>Inshaw's Steam Packet</u>

In addition to the horse-drawn packet service, there was also a steam packet at weekends, which was introduced through the inventiveness of John Inshaw. He was a man of many parts. He was associated with the 'Steam Clock' public house and also Paper Mills in Cheston Road, Aston (later acquired by Smith, Stone & Knight).

A trial trip in August 1843 travelled 4 miles from Icknield Street Bridge and carried 80 passengers. It was a steam powered paddle boat; paddles were arranged in front of vessel to enable it to pass through locks and avoid contact with other boats.

John Inshaw ran his steam packet boat *Phoenix* from Broad Street Bridge to Bilston Street Bridge, Wolverhampton, initially on Sunday only. The Birmingham Journal of 14 September 1844 refers to the boat leaving Birmingham at 9 a.m., returning from Wolverhampton at 5 p.m. Fare 1s each way.

Inshaw's boats may have outlived the Swift Packet service, but the explosion of the *Fury* at Tipton is believed to have contributed to the service ceasing for good. In 1856, Mr Inshaw's boats again saw use, taking passengers to the 'fetes' at Aston Hall.

The drawing is based on publicity

Galton Bridge - though the boats are not packet boats!

advertisements for Shipton's Swift Packet published in 1843. It shows the boat passing under Galton Bridge. The bridge, in the distance, was also shown in the Swift Packet advert, and would appear to depict the original Spon Lane Bridge. The Packet boat is therefore shown to be travelling from Birmingham to Wolverhampton.

Q is for *Quail*

The merchandise carrying boat service was as old as the canals along which it plied. In the early days, the horse was the chief means of power. Horse drawn craft passed along the waterways of Britain at a steady rate, calling at the many wharves and providing a timetabled collection and delivery service. Speed was a finite factor, as boats rarely travelled above three miles an hour. Journey times could be reduced by restricting the number of calling points and by travelling both day and night, until the final destination was reached. The latter option was adopted by most merchandise carriers and was popularly known as the 'fly-boat'. The slower 'stage-boat' called at all points and acted often as feeders for the fly-boats.

Shropshire Union Fly-Boat.

Experiments with steam-powered craft eventually produced a boat that was powerful enough to tow another, as well as carrying a load itself. Faster journeys became possible without the hampering infrastructure of providing the frequent change of horses and stabling. The steamers were also more versatile; they could travel through tunnels without recourse to legging, and they could also pass more easily along arms and into basins reducing, therefore, the need for poling.

Fellows, Morton & Clayton Ltd became an important force in canal carrying following the merger that created the firm in 1889. Subsequent mergers and takeovers increased their grip on the inland trade. FMC were not the only carrier to use steamboats, but became the biggest operator of this type on the narrow canals. A principal disadvantage of the FMC steamers was that the engine and boiler took up valuable cargo space. The development of the motorboat powered by the internal combustion engine gave greater cargo space and produced the most versatile craft yet seen on inland navigation.

Quail was a wooden hulled motorboat, which belonged to the canal carriers Fellows, Morton & Clayton. She was built at the

FMC Boatyard at Uxbridge in 1916 and fitted with a 10 hp Bolinder engine. *Quail* was registered in the Birmingham Sanitary Authority list as no 1348, on 28 July 1916. James Sadler was recorded as the captain, or master.

The use of motorboats on inland navigations undoubtedly prolonged the life of general canal carrying, and those that survive provide a lasting reminder of those days. Although various types of motor were made available for canal boats, the Swedish manufactured Bolinder engine was the choice preferred by Fellows, Morton & Clayton Ltd. Up to the year 1911, FMC continued to build steamers. Following the example of others, FMC decided to fit a new boat with a Bolinder engine. Their first trial boat was the *Linda*, which was commissioned in April 1912 (Registered in Birmingham No 1256, 3 May 1912).

Quail was numbered 109 in the FMC fleet, and was the eighteenth motorboat built for this firm of canal carriers. Many were of iron composite construction. That is, they had an iron hull, but traditional wood bottom. Those made at Uxbridge were constructed completely from wood.

The use of internal combustion engines for canal transport on the narrow canals of the West Midlands began with the trials of the NB *Duchess* in January 1906. This craft had a Thorneycroft Gas Engine on board, which used suction gas provided by a gas producer plant. The *Duchess* spent some 3 months traversing the midland waterway network, but little is heard of her after this.

Thorneycroft's gas powered barge trials, however, provided a spur to others. The magazine 'Motor Traction' printed a full-page article in their issue of 15 December 1906, entitled 'Motor Barge Development on Canals', where the NB *Progress* was described. The author of the piece observed that although motorised barges had seen considerable development on the continent, the English canal barge proprietors had not seen their way to adopt the motor for transport purposes. The general 'bad' state of British Canals was attributed to the lack of enterprise. NB *Progress* had been built by Norman Tailby (for Edward Tailby, timber merchants) of King Edward's Road, Birmingham, and was fitted with a 16 hp two-cylinder paraffin engine made by Gardner of Manchester. The engine was run at 600 rpm and a special type of magneto ignition had been fitted. According to her gauging record (BCN 11602, gauged 21 September 1907), the *Progress* was 71ft 6in long by 7ft 1in broad.

Progress had already been tested on the local canals. It was sent into South Staffordshire and returned with a full load of bricks. It then went from Birmingham to Gloucester with a full load and returned with 24 tons of timber. A further article appeared in 'Motor Traction' of 24 August 1907, which describes NB *Progress* belonging to Edward Tailby. In this piece, the engine is said to be 15hp. On the previous Saturday, the *Progress* had made a trip on the Birmingham & Worcester Canal. A number of guests had been invited on board for a trip from Breedon Cross to Tardebigge. During the trip, Norman Tailby, who had built the boat, described some of the recent journeys undertaken. *Progress* had made trips to Sharpness, a distance of 97 miles, taking six days to complete the return journey. 25 tons of deal had been loaded for the outward trip, but the vessel had returned empty. Another journey was made from Birmingham to Ellesmere Port, a distance of 85 miles. This return trip was also accomplished in 6 days. The outward part took a mixed cargo including bedsteads and the return journey was with a load of timber. The boat travelled at an average speed of 5-6 miles per hour. Running costs including tolls etc., averaged ¾d per ton per mile. Normal paraffin costing 5d a gallon was used.

The use of motorboats and tugs on inland waterways increased after 1920, and came to be adopted by all general canal carriers. *Quail*, it seems, was regularly used by FMC on the London trade, travelling from the Midlands along the Grand Junction Canal into the heart of the metropolis. It was customary to pair boats together as they worked through the double locks on this route. *Quail* was at one time paired with the unpowered 'butty' *Bascote* (Registered Birmingham 1522, August 1929).

Wooden boats have a finite life and although cheaper to build than iron boats (*Quail* cost £450), they required more maintenance. *Quail's* original Bolinder was replaced with more powerful 15hp version in 1925 and she was extensively rebuilt at Uxbridge between 1940 and 1941.

When Fellows, Morton & Clayton ceased carrying and filed for liquidation in 1949, *Quail* passed into the hands of the Docks and Inland Waterways Executive. She was purchased by Willow Wren Canal Carrying Company in 1954, and paired for a time with the *Kingfisher*. Following the general cessation of canal carrying, *Quail* survived and went from mooring to mooring until she finally ended up on the Kennet and Avon Canal. She was broken up at Devizes during the autumn of 2000!

Edward Paget Tomlinson's drawing depicts the *Quail* on the BCN main line, a journey she may have undertaken from time to time, and one which is certain if she was ever attached the North West fleet. When she first entered service, Fellows, Morton & Clayton had local depots in Birmingham (Fazeley Street & Bordesley Street), Dudley Port (Grand Junction Wharf) and

Wolverhampton (Albion Wharf). Probable excursions into this area would include the collection of iron goods or the delivery of grain or timber. *Quail* is shown being gauged at the island toll office, Winson Green, which was located on the main line from Birmingham to Wolverhampton. The toll clerk is seen busy taking measurements with his gauging stick, which he would then check with the gauging tables to verify the cargo weight.

Fellows, Morton & Clayton motor boat *Quail*.

Bromford Stop Toll Office, Spon Lane, 1950s. *Bob May Collection*

The same toll office as on the previous page. George Arnold and horse Betty, with CEA day boat.   *Graham Guest*

Two views of Winson Green stop, after demolition of the toll office.   *Brenda Ward*

R is for Rushall

Modern Rushall is now part of Walsall, but there was a time when it was a separate community with its own identity. The Parish of Rushall was predominantly agricultural, but there was some industry, which included a number of limestone mines. The Daw End Branch of the Wyrley and Essington Canal ran through the district and served the limestone mines at Daw End and the Quarries at Hay Head. The physical end of the Daw End Branch passed out of Rushall to terminate a few yards within Walsall. It was here that the Hay Head Quarries were located, which were prized for a particular quality of hydraulic lime.

For some forty-six years the Daw End Canal was simply a branch waterway that served the limestone works of Rushall and the brickyards of Aldridge. In 1847, a new canal was opened that joined the Daw End Canal with the Tame Valley Canal at Newton Junction. This new link was named the Rushall Canal, although only a short piece was actually within Rushall Parish.

The Rushall Canal was built in an age when Acts of Parliament more frequently sanctioned railway construction than canals. It was part of a group of new waterways constructed for the BCN that forged additional connections between the Wyrley & Essington and BCN systems. During the 1820s and 1830s, several proposals were made to improve canal communications in this area, both by the BCN and others intending to establish rival canals. Finally the BCN committee set their surveyors to plan a line of canal along the Tame Valley and also form a junction canal with the Daw End branch.

An initial proposal was rejected in favour of the route which was finally adopted. These proposals were already in place when the BCN and Wyrley & Essington Canals merged in 1840. Parliamentary approval was sought and granted, and work went ahead with the construction of the Bentley, Rushall and Tame Valley Canals. Contracts were let for the Bentley and Tame Valley, and work concentrated on these projects first. It seems the contract for the Rushall Canal was not let until 1844, when new fresh capital had been raised to complete the Tame Valley and build the Rushall. The contractors Frost and Bate were awarded the contract. The 'Frost' was Matthew Frost, of Bilston, who was involved in both canal and railway building projects. The BCN, for their part had to cleanse and deepen the lower part of the Daw End Branch.

Traffic along the newly opened Rushall Canal would have included bricks, coal and limestone, which was the traditional trade of the Daw End Canal. However the limestone trade declined with the exhaustion and closure of some of the mines. New coal traffic more than compensated for this loss, when the Cannock Chase Coalfield was developed during the 1860s. Coal traffic on this waterway was increased further with the sinking of new mines near Aldridge and Walsall Wood. This was a period when coal was still essential to the workings of industry. Boat after boat would pass up and down, taking coal to the many canal side wharves and loading places dotted around the West Midlands.

The Rushall Canal is 2 miles and 6½ furlongs long, and connects the Walsall Level (406ft) with the Wolverhampton Canal (473ft). Nine locks raise the boats from the level at Newton Junction to Longwood Junction, where the Rushall Canal joins the Daw End Branch. Seven locks are placed close together, but then there is a level section before the other two locks at Longwood. Here the canal still passes through the fields. It is an exposed location where winds often lash at the passing boats.

No industry was established along this route, and the only wharf was at the Bell Inn. The Bell Wharf was a public wharf and there was also stabling at the Inn for the boatmens' horses. The main features of canal interest were simply the locks, company cottages and the bridges. At Longwood, beside the top lock, were the tollhouse and a stable.

Boatmen have a tendency to label places and objects with their own terms. Thus the boats they worked were affectionately called 'joeys' or 'joshers' and nicknames such as the 'Crow' and 'Ganzey' applied to sections of the waterway. A Ganzey was a term for a jumper, or pullover [derived from Guernsey, a seaman's pullover]. In canal slang, the boatmen sometimes called the cold windswept places Ganzeys symbolising their need to wear warmer clothing there. The Rushall was popularly known as the Ganzey for this reason.

Edward Paget Tomlinson's drawing shows the top lock and office at Longwood with a typical coal boat passing into the lock. The drawing depicts the boat *Nil Desperandum*, which belonged to Stephen Stephens of Smethwick. According to Edward, Stephens' boats were docked at Peter Keay's Dock at Daw End, and it would be reasonable to see them passing Longwood from time to time.

During the Second World War, Longwood Top Lock also had a tearoom where tea was provided for the passing boatmen. The role of the waterways during this time is often undervalued, and the canals did sterling service. The movement of coal was essential to keep the wheels of industry moving.

The GEC [General Electric Company], at Witton, was an important canal customer, whose role was essential to the war effort. There was a powerhouse at Witton that burnt a lot of coal, all of which came in by canal boat. Further along the 'cut' was Nechells 'A' power station that also had a voracious appetite for coal. There were rolling mills, foundries and press shops that all relied on the coal getting through.

A BCN at war held many differences from that in peacetime. Visible from the waterway would be gun sites and barrage balloons. May be aircraft would pass overhead on test flights from Castle Bromwich Aerodrome. There were strategic places where stop planks could be inserted and members of the Home Guard manned these, day and night, in case there was a breach. The Fire Service also made provisions for extracting water from the canal and special doorways were put into bridges to aid this purpose. The Canal Company headquarters was even moved from the centre of Birmingham to Sneyd.

Bombing damaged the BCN network, particularly during the years of 1940 and 1941. Rubble from fallen buildings obstructed towpaths, and had to be cleared away. Locks were hit and needed repair. Alternative traffic routes were essential to keep trade flowing. Canals such as the Rushall provided those alternatives. Those tea ladies at Longwood were kept very busy in many ways.

Coal traffic continued after the war, but changes in industrial practice, as well as the closure of many local collieries, reduced trade on the Ganzey from a flow to a trickle. Eventually even this trickle stopped.

The future of the canal may have looked bleak were it not for the boaters who established a base at Longwood. A portion of the Daw End Canal continued past Longwood Junction to the Hay Head Quarries. These quarries had been long disused (some sources suggest by the mid 1850s) and this section of the waterway had become clogged with weed. In 1931 Walsall Corporation had dropped Hay Bridge that carried Longwood Lane over the canal, rendering the quarries completely inaccessible to canal boats. A boat club was formed at Longwood that utilised the banks of the main canal around the junction and later dug out the arm as far as Longwood Lane for use as residential moorings.

This section of the BCN does not see the boating traffic as other parts of the system, yet those wishing to pass this way might find it a rewarding experience. Parts of the Tame Valley, Rushall and Daw End are tree lined. There are deep cuttings and high embankments. There are also many contrasts, as the straight lined waterways of nineteenth century engineering skills give way to meandering canals formed in the eighteenth century.

Lock cottage 192 by Rushall Lock No. 3, 1960s.
BCN Archives

Lock cottage 193 by Rushall top lock, alongside Longwood Boat Club, formerly stables, 2002. The bridge did not exist until built in 2001 by BW. *Brenda Ward*

The Rushall Canal joined the Tame Valley Canal at Rushall, or Newton, Junction and the entrance to the Rushall Canal was spanned by a side bridge that carried the west side towpath over the waterway. In the distance is a another footbridge, Brickfields Bridge, that united both towpaths and enabled horses to cross from the east side towpath in order to work boats along the Rushall Canal and the single towpath that extended to the Daw End Canal at Longwood Junction.

Left, and above - Caggy Stevens and horse Bonnie at Rushall with coal from Cannock Wood/Anglesey Basin.

S is for Steward Aqueduct

Those who travel by train from Birmingham to Wolverhampton along the Stour Valley Railway are provided with ample opportunity to look at the Birmingham Canal main line from the comfort of a train seat. It is a view that has been available to people since the railway was first opened to passenger trains in 1852, and offers a unique perspective for the canal from Smethwick through to Bilston. There have been many changes along the route since the day the passenger trains commenced running, most important being the disappearance of the canal side buildings and industry.

A set of photographs was taken from a train window that captures the view as it was in 1947. These pictures, which were published in a book called 'Conurbation', represent a very different scene than that which can be seen today.

The drawing is based on one image from this collection, which was the view from the window when the train passed through Spon Lane. It shows the Wolverhampton Level of the BCN (473ft o.d.) and the Steward Aqueduct that carried this canal over the Birmingham Level (453ft o.d.) near Spon Lane Glassworks. The boat shown in the drawing about to pass over the aqueduct is the Thomas Clayton tar boat, *Gifford*, which at one time was owned by Edward Paget-Tomlinson. Tar boats were common sights on the local waterways, where they frequently carried tar and ammoniacal liquor from the gasworks to the chemical works. There was a concentration of these chemical works in the Oldbury district, and in this view *Gifford* would have been heading for one of these works or Clayton's Dock there.

Tar boats were constructed to a distinctive design where the hold was enclosed to contain two tanks that were filled with the liquid being carried. Although some tar boats were motor powered in later years, others such as *Gifford* remained horse drawn. Conventional horse boats left space in the hold for feed for the horse, but tar boats could not store fodder in this fashion and kept it on the deck in a special pyramid shaped container.

This view of the Steward Aqueduct also shows a line of canal side cottages that were placed beside a footpath that linked the towpaths of both levels. There was a towpath across the aqueduct on both sides, which was unusual for the upper canal. The Wolverhampton Level at this point comprised the original 'Old' main line that was opened in stages through to Aldersley between 1770 and 1772. According to Brindley's original survey, a tunnel should have been made to take the canal through the hillside here, but this plan was amended during construction and the route was taken over the hillside by a set of locks that rose to the summit at 490 ft before descending to the Birmingham level again. Spon Lane marked the junction between the 'main' line to Wolverhampton and the 'branch' canal to the coalmines at Hill Top (Wednesbury Canal). The canals diverged at the pound situated between the 9th and 10th locks. Canal improvements reduced the summit to the Wolverhampton Level, in 1790, and created a new summit level from Smethwick to Wolverhampton at the 473 ft level. Three locks remained at Spon Lane to take the waterway down for the Wednesbury Canal and the later extensions to Walsall. Placed in the junction between Spon Lane Top Lock and the main line was a BCN tollhouse and cottage.

Further canal improvements made between 1826 and 1829 led to the construction of the New Main Line, engineered by Thomas Telford and site engineer William McKenzie. Thomas Townshend was the main contractor for the work. An aqueduct was constructed to carry the 'Old' main line over the 'New' main line. At the same time, the route of the Old Main was altered a few yards to the west. The aqueduct crossing was made at an angle to the New Main Line and is composite of brick, stone and metal.

One result of the diversion was that some three acres of canal land and former canal bed was given up to Chance Brothers and later incorporated into the Spon Lane Glassworks site. It was on 18 May 1824 that Robert Lucas Chance had purchased the glassworks of the British Crown-Glass

Steward Aqueduct in 1967.

Company at Spon Lane, and gradually extended the works across a square of land bounded on one side by 'Old' main line, to which basin accommodation enabled raw material to be brought by boat and finished glass in crates despatched in the same manner.

Glassmaking at Spon Lane was dependent on a supply of flint sands, alkali, limestone and coal, all of which came to the works by canal. Chance Brothers continued the manufacture of Crown glass, which was a square pane with a circular thickened bulls-eye. Such glass was commonly used in the windows of more affluent properties. The production of Crown Glass was a wasteful process and was gradually replaced by Sheet Glass. Chance and Hartley copied a German method and commenced making 'Bohemian' sheet glass in 1832, but did not perfect the process until some six years later. The Spon Lane works were enlarged in consequence, and continued to be enlarged as more work was taken on. They extended their works on to the slope of the (north) embankment that led down to the BCN New Main Line, erecting shops almost to the edge of the towpath. Despite a lengthy closure process, these building remain, even if they are in an increasingly fragile state.

Chance Brothers later commenced making sheet rolled plate glass and also produced specialist glasses such as lighthouse glass. Their works was further extended to land on the opposite side of the New Main Line (south) embankment.

The Stour Valley Railway, constructed between 1848 and 1851, runs parallel to the towpath of the New Main Line at Spon Lane, but at a higher level. The railway proprietors having elected to take their railway close to the banks of the BCN, found a restricted passage at Spon Lane where the railway was confined to a strip of canal land that formed the (south) embankment. Contractors built up the level of the railway, and a tall retaining wall was made to contain the Stour Valley Railway and separate it from the canal. The railway was built at such a height to enable it to pass over the Old Main Line at one end of the Steward Aqueduct. Spon Lane railway interchange basin was made on the other side of the railway embankment, which was opened for traffic in 1852. Here goods were exchanged between canal boats and railway wagons.

Steward Aqueduct is a substantial structure that is supported by two arches that span the lower New Main Line Canal. Only one of these arches is depicted in the drawing and the view from the train window has changed considerably since the 1940s. An elevated section of the M5 motorway now passes above both canals and railway, making a four-tier layer of transport at this spot.

The Steward Aqueduct after the M5 motorway had been built.

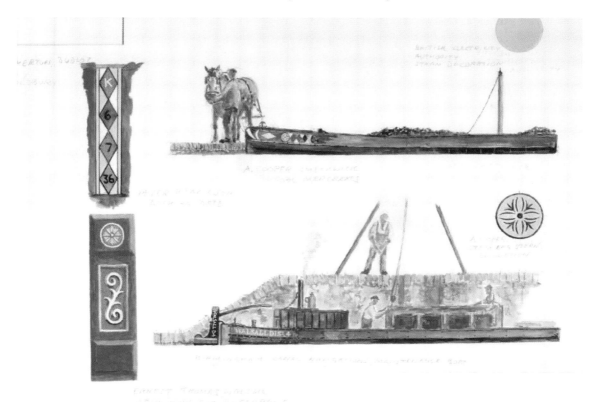

Some of Edward Paget-Tomlinson's paintings for his book 'Colours of the Cut'.
Top - Horse drawn day boat - A Cooper, coal merchant, Smethwick.
Bottom - BCN maintenance boat.

T is for Titford

Most motorists who travel along the elevated section of the M5, in the Midlands, are unaware of the canal network hidden below the motorway. A forest of supports form a concrete cocoon around a long section of the Birmingham Canal (Old Main Line) and a small canal reservoir known as Titford Pools. The remnants of the reservoir at Titford are amongst the oldest surviving features of the old Birmingham Canal. The pools date from the period between 1773 and 1774 when a dam was raised to enclose a nine acre site.

The following advertisement was published in Aris's Birmingham Gazette on July 21, 1783:

BIRMINGHAM CANAL NAVIGATION
GREAT Numbers of Persons having of late made a Practice of ANGLING, and otherwise Fishing in the Reservoirs at Smethwick and Titford, belonging to the Company: Notice is hereby given, That all Persons who shall be found trespassing in future, will be prosecuted with the utmost Rigour; and likewise all Persons, who after this Notice, shall be seen Bathing, or sending Dogs in the Canal.
JOHN MEREDITH, Clerk to the Proprietors.

Over two hundred years have passed since the publication of this notice, but Titford still retains a role as a reservoir that supplies the Birmingham Canal Navigations and other associated waterways. Titford Reservoir ranked with the Great Smethwick Reservoirs as an early supplier of water to the Navigation, but although the need for Smethwick Reservoir was swept away by Telford's water supply improvements made during the period 1825-1830, Titford Reservoir was retained and linked by a new feeder to Edgbaston Reservoir.

Titford Reservoir collects water from the hills above Rowley Regis. These same hills also provide water for the embryonic River Tame that flows through the heart of the Black Country, and once provided power for a number of water mills placed strategically along its length. Telford's feeder was a narrow channel that replaced the original feeder link to the Old Birmingham Canal. Its engineering was just as complex as any navigable canal: embankments, cuts, tunnels and bridges were required. It even crossed Stoney Lane near the Blue Gates, Smethwick by a cast-iron aqueduct.

The Titford end of this feeder had but a brief existence as a narrow channel before plans were being made to widen it for navigation and link it to the Old BCN by a flight of six locks. The reasons behind this work were to enable boats to reach the coalmines being developed in the Oldbury Valley. Some mines were already accessible by tramroad links down to wharves beside the Old Main Line, but a canal link promised better access to new mines then being sunk. Alternate routes were discussed but the final solution was the line from Oldbury through to Titford Pools that involved the flight of six locks.

BCN Committee Minutes for February 1835 record a letter from Thomas Bartlett, who was agent to a Mr Willets. Willets had sunk shafts to coal measures, but these mines lacked suitable canal facilities. The BCN, who were already planning a branch in the area, were able to reply that they were about to apply to Parliament in order to make a branch according to a plan arranged by W. Fowler. The route was to leave their existing canal near Stoney Lane Bridge and then climb through locks to join the feeder. The feeder would then be made navigable to Titford Pools. There would be two branches, one to the Portway Road beyond the Pools, whilst the other was to run to the West side of the valley.

The plans for building the canal were finalised by November 1835, when it was decided that it should be made to a top width of 30ft, a depth of 5ft and the slopes to be inclined at 1½ to 1.

Work on construction went ahead through 1836 and 1837 on the canal, locks and feeder improvements. Work on the Portway Branch meant that the canal line had to cross in front, or over, the old reservoir dam in some fashion. The Titford Canal was opened to traffic from 4 October 1837, and opened up a new canal communication to the brick works and coal mines around Portway and Newberry Lane. The so called western branch was evidently not built at this date. This section of waterway was finally completed as the Causeway Green Branch, and was finished during 1858. The Causeway Green Canal enabled mines such as Cakemore and Rowley Station to send coal by canal.

Once completed in 1837, this line reached the highest navigable level on the BCN, at 511 ft (o.d.). Some three years later, when the BCN merged with the Wyrley & Essington Canal Company, a higher navigation, the Essington Branch Canal came under BCN control, but this waterway had ceased to be used following mine closures and, in effect, Titford has remained the highest BCN navigation to this day. Another potential candidate for the highest BCN navigation could have gone to the Dudley Canal Company, who proposed a flight of locks up from the Bumble Hole to the Buffery Collieries near Dudley. Carey's Map

(1796) suggests there might have been as many as ten locks, which on an average rise of 6 feet from the Dudley No. 2 canal at 453ft, might have also reached a similar height to Titford. The Buffery Branch was abandoned, on Thomas Dadford's recommendations, in favour of a tramway, but it still conjures up pictures of what might have been. Titford may be the highest navigable waterway in the Midlands, but it no longer has the honour of being the highest in England; that honour must now pass to the restored Huddersfield Narrow Canal, which rises to a navigable summit of 645ft.

With the building of Titford Locks and the widening of the feeder for boat navigation, the need for water conservation was immediately considered. Whilst construction of the locks was underway, tenders were sent out for a pumping engine to recirculate water between the 473ft level, at Oldbury, and the 511 ft Titford Level. Boulton & Watt won the contract to supply a single-acting beam engine, which was erected in a house built between the top lock and the 4½-mile long feeder link to Edgbaston Reservoir. A single boiler was erected in an adjoining structure; later a second boiler was provided. A close study of the Oldbury Tithe map appears to show that both buildings were aligned one behind the other.

The carriage of coal may have provided the incentive for the construction of the waterway, but other cargoes such as chemicals, phosphates, oil and tar were later to become important commodities carried along the Titford Canal. The development of Albright & Wilson's phosphorus works would bring significant toll revenue to the canal, as would the later establishment of British Cyanides.

For some reason, Titford Locks became known as the 'Jim Crow'. There was also an arm or basin called the Jim Crow that joined the canal at the pound between the third and fourth lock. This branch is absent from the tithe map (1857), and appears have been built to accommodate the Phosphorus Works extensions made during the 1860s. The branch name would then be derived from the name by which the lock flight was already known. This becomes apparent when the text of a letter published as early as February 1856, in the Birmingham Journal is considered. The author signed it with the word an 'Observer':

Sir, - I think that purchasers of coal from the collieries along the Titford Canal ought to be made aware of the extent to which depredations are carried out all along the "Jim Crow" Locks. I am a daily observer of these depredations and cannot pass over such things in silence. I see enormous lumps of the best coal thrown out by the boatman in considerable quantities onto the side of the locks, as the boats are passing through, and thence carried to the adjoining houses by women, boys and girls....

As traffic on the Titford Canal increased, demand for additional pumping power became an urgent requirement. It was decided to purchase an additional pumping engine, which also involved the sinking of a parallel pumping shaft. The engine house was also reconstructed at the same time, whereby the original and second engines were located side by side in adjacent engine halls. The second engine was erected between 1863 and 1864. It was a beam engine made by G & J Davis of Tipton that was purchased second-hand from the South Staffordshire Waterworks Company.

At some later date, a blacksmith shop, in a lean-to building, was made alongside the engine house facing the lock side.

Both engines were retained at Titford until the traffic decline of the 1920s. The Boulton and Watt engine was cut up in 1928, whilst the Davis engine was scrapped in 1937. A Tangye Oil Engine replaced them, from 1928, which remained here until 1965.

The drawing reflects a time before the steam boilers had been taken out of use. A boat is shown in the top lock chamber, whilst another lies tied up on the feeder arm loaded with coal for the boilers. A short section of the feeder beyond the engine house had been made navigable to supply the Titford engines. Later, the navigation was extended as far as Adams coal yard and the BIP (former British Cyanides) Chemical Works. In some accounts, the name for this navigable section is given as the Tat Bank, or Spon Lane, Branch. BCN distance tables simply refer to it as a feeder. There were other canal side buildings not shown in this view, including a canal house and stable block that lined the towpath near the top lock.

Some of the last traffic on the branch included coal to Langley Forge from Cannock Chase. All local mines had long since closed and loaded coal boats passed up the 'Crow', rather than down it. When this traffic ceased in the 1960s, the Titford Canal quickly became overgrown and weeded. Were it not for the 1970s clean up campaign and subsequent boat rallies, the future of the waterway might have the suffered the same fate as the Ridgeacre and become closed to navigation for good.

Fortunately members of the BCN Society, IWA and other local groups each played a part in preserving a portion of BCN heritage. It has not been possible to stop the loss of certain structures such as the stables and canal house, which have both been demolished, but the engine houses are veteran survivors. Despite a serious arson attack, the buildings were refurbished by British Waterways in 2001, to provide residential accommodation, a meeting room, boaters, facilities and a new pump room. Whilst reconstruction was underway, it was possible to see how the buildings were put together. The engine house nearer the Tat Bank Branch was evidently older than that nearer the lock side, and there was a large bricked up archway that may have formed a communication between the two halls. It was decided not to restore the boiler house at the rear, and the structure was partially taken down. When the boiler house wharf below the top lock was cleansed of rubbish, a short brick arched tunnel was discovered, which may have been used to convey the ashes from the boiler to a boat moored beside the wharf.

Even at this late stage, the Titford Pump House had secrets to give up. It is also a remarkable achievement that a nineteenth century structure has found a new role as part of a twenty-first century waterway. So many more buildings are lost to the planner's whim. Titford Pools are a prime example of planner's dreams. When 'Conurbation' was published in the 1940s, an artist touched up a picture of the pools to show them filled with sailing yachts and people swimming. Such were the immediate post-war hopes. The planners of the M5 motorway were to end this dream. The elevated motorway neatly bisects the Pools, its concrete supports sunk deep into the bed of the reservoir!

Paintings by Edward Paget-Tomlinson -

Details of boat decoration, and cabin door.

A rather unhappy scene in 1988 - a derelict Titford pumphouse, before renovation.   *Mike Rolfe*

Titford, 1950.   *Weaver Collection, HNBC*

Titford, 2012.

U is for Union Mill

The grinding of flour from corn to make bread had been confined to wind or water mills, but once steam power was adapted to turn the mill stones, the dependence on wind power or waterpower was removed forever. Flour mills were relocated at the centres of population where the need for bread was greatest. The banks of the BCN had a number of flour mills, where the canal provided the means of transport for grain and coal.

Sufficient finance was required to build a steam driven mill. Joint stock companies established several mills where funds were provided by shareholders. These mills were more than simple places to grind wheat and corn into flour. They were also bakeries that produced bread in quantity. All were tall buildings comprising four or five stories. Edward Paget-Tomlinson's drawing depicts Union Mill at Wolverhampton. The brickwork rises out of the bed of the canal dwarfing the boats moored alongside. These boats had brought grain in sacks for grinding into flour.

Union Mill was one of a group of corn mills placed beside the Birmingham Canal near Horseleyfields. It started production in 1813, and was seemingly the first there. At least Melville's Wolverhampton Directory (1851) states that Union Mill was established about 1812, financed by 14,000 shares of £1 each. The tasks of finance and construction took about a year, as is indicated by the following advertisement that appeared in Aris's Gazette on 20 September 1813.

Wolverhampton Flour and Bread Company
September 17, 1813

In Consequence of the Subscribers being permitted to hold forty shares each, the Demand has exceeded Expectation.
To complete so great an Undertaking, a large Sum has been necessarily expended; yet after making that Deduction, together with the Money requisite to finish and set to Work the Mill and Bakehouse, there remains a balance of 2600l. With this Sum, and supported by the Credit of the Committee, the Mill will be put in motion in a few Days.

The Shares are limited to 15,000, nearly thirteen are already subscribed; therefore an Opportunity remains for those who wish to participate in a concern so laudable.

As the Flour and Bread Company have no Views beyond attempting to cause that important Article, Bread, to be made wholesome, and to be procured on the lowest Terms, the Justice of the Cause induced them to treat with silent Contempt the fallacious Advertisements circulated by an interested Party.

By Order of the Committee
THOMAS SYMCOX, Clerk

Union Mill was erected on land near to Union Wharf, the carrying depot for Crowley & Company, and formed part of a growing number of buildings that came to line the waterfront there. By 1816, Joseph Norton was operating another mill nearby that was called the Old Steam Mill. Edward Harrold owned a third called Horseley Mill. During the 1830s a fourth mill, Albion Mill, was in work and owned by James Bradshaw.

Canal side flour mills and bakeries provided an essential service to the growing local population. The merchandise canal carriers transported imported grain from ports such as Gloucester and Liverpool to the mills, whilst local grown cereals often came to the mill by road.

Birmingham had the greatest concentration of combined steam powered mills and bakeries. The first was the Old Union Mill, which was established beside the Digbeth Branch in the 1797. The Birmingham Union Mill, in Holt Street, was the first flour mill to be built alongside the banks of the BCN. It was established by the Birmingham Flour & Bread Company that was formed in June 1796. The preamble of their articles of association provides the principal reason for the creation of the mill that both ground wheat, but also baked the flour to make bread. This company was formed during troubled times when food was expensive. Established bakers were criticised for adulterating the bread they made, and the following is a reproduction from the text:

Whereas from various Causes and Circumstances, the Price of Flour and Bread is risen to an unexampled and exorbitant Height, and the different Classes of Society have been most shamefully imposed upon by various People, in grinding almost all kinds of Grain and mixing thereof with Wheaten Flour; and the several Persons and parties hereto, feeling with Indignation such Impositions, and fearing, that unless some proper and effectual Means are taken, the Evil amending the high Price of Grain, and the shameful Adulteration of Flour may continue; and being of the opinion, that nothing can tend more effectually to remedy the same, than forming themselves into a Society, Company,

Union Mill, Wolverhampton - before destroyed by fire.

or Copartnership, for the Purpose of erecting a Mill, or Mills, Store Rooms, Bake Houses and other Buildings, and for buying Corn, grinding thereof, making Part of the same, into Bread, and distributing of or dealing in Flour and Bread.

The subscription was not to exceed £20,000 in £1 shares. Each shareholder was entitled to buy a weekly amount of bread and, or, flour. Union Mill, Birmingham, commenced work on 18 August 1797 grinding wheat brought from the Birmingham market and other sources within a twenty miles radius of the mill. In addition to catering for shareholder needs, the mill supplied loaves of bread to the Asylum, Hospital, Soup Shop and Barracks. The mill property comprised the mill complete with millstones and dressing machines, the bakery, engine house and a canal wharf beside the Digbeth Branch of the BCN.

Four stones were provided for the mill, although only three were generally in use at any one time. The bakery comprised five ovens and generally four ovens were used for baking at a time. The annual consumption of coal was about 400 tons, which equates to only a boatload every three weeks.

Steam-powered mill construction increased during the nineteenth century. Birmingham had the largest concentration. Albion Mill was established beside the Newhall Branch about 1803 and then the New Union Mill, on the Old Main Line was opened during 1813. There were three mills below the locks at Farmer's Bridge. Two were in Snow Hill, one was known as Old Steam Mill, and the other as

Eagle Flour Mill. A third in Princip Street was called the Britannia Mill. One of the Snow Hill mills, perhaps the Old Steam Mill, was also known as the Salutation Mill. There were also a small mill, known as Central, on the Digbeth Branch near Belmont Row, a mill in Summer Row close to Friday Bridge, and the Midland Flour Mill, on the New Main Line near St Vincent Street. Once the New Union Mill was opened the original Union Mill became known as the Old Union Mill.

Joint stock companies did not own all canal side mills; some were family ventures. The Pratt family was, at one time, associated with mills at Bloxwich, Ettingshall and Stoke on Trent. They also established a merchandise canal carrying business. Pratt's Mill, Bloxwich, was erected beside the Wyrley & Essington Canal. The Ettingshall Mill (commonly called the Bilston & Sedgley Mill) was a large building with its own basin that ran under the mill, and connected with the main line of the BCN. The basin was used for both loading and unloading purposes. In 1834, Ettingshall Mill was powered by a 45hp steam engine. French and Derby millstones were used to grind the grain and there were four dressing machines capable of dressing upwards of 1200 sacks per week. Several ovens were erected on premises to bake on a large scale.

Tipton had two flour mills. One was placed beside the Old Main Line near Owen Street, and was sometimes referred to as the Tipton Green Mill, and also the Dudley & Tipton Mill. The second mill, another Union Mill, was located beside the Tipton Green Locks. There was a mill beside the old BCN at Canalside, Oldbury, whilst Nock's Mill at Great Bridge stood close to the Walsall Canal. There were several flour mills in Walsall, but not all were canal served. The most notable is Albion Mill that stands beside the Walsall Locks Branch. Trade directories also record a Birchills Steam Mill, which may have been near the canal. Some mills had a relatively short existence. Those at French Walls, Smethwick were offered for sale in 1813. Boulton & Watt purchased the mill and later converted the premises into an iron and steelworks.

Competition from modern mills equipped with up to date machinery and changes in bread making techniques affected the profitability of the steam mills, and many closed after 1900. The Wolverhampton Union Mill stopped milling during the early 1900s, but nearby Norton's Mill under the proprietorship of J N Miller would continue in production for most of the twentieth century. Another long-lived mill was Albion Mill, Walsall, which closed down relatively recently.

Canal traffic to the surviving mills ceased many years ago. The last carriers to bring grain to the mills were Fellows, Morton & Clayton, and the Midlands & Coast Carrying Company. The Midlands & Coast boats brought wheat from Ellesmere Port to

Bloxwich (Pratt's) Mill and took the empty sacks back. Fellows, Morton & Clayton carried grain to both the Midland Mill and Old Union Mill in Birmingham.

Few flour mills remain today. Union Mill, Wolverhampton, remained standing for most of the twentieth century, but was destroyed by fire, a common fate for old flour mills. Those that survive are the Albion Mill at Wolverhampton, the Albion Mill, Walsall and Union Mill, Tipton.

Norton's Mill in Wolverhampton was demolished very recently. It been standing idle for a number of years. The building was extensively rebuilt after a serious fire in 1851. The original structure had been built beside the main line of the BCN, but with the construction of Wolverhampton Queen Street/Central Station the main line was diverted on to another route and Norton's Mill was left beside a stub of the old canal. When the mill was rebuilt, the mill building was extended over the waterway fronting Corn Hill.

Union Mill,
Wolverhampton.
*Chris Hall, courtesy
of Julie Wilkinson*

V is for Valentia Wharf

The name Valencia Wharf is known to every owner of an Allen Brothers boat as the yard where their boat was constructed. Placed beside the Old Main Line at Oldbury near Whimsey Bridge, the Allen Boatyard was a seemingly enduring feature until the Allen Brothers decided to retire and close the yard in 1997. Les Allen had learnt the trade building and repairing the Joey and Cabin boats at Salford Bridge, for Spencer Abbot, but later transferred to Oldbury about 1951, where he traded as Les Allen & Sons. Bob and Tom Allen assisted their father to build and repair boats in the yard that had previously been used by Thomas & Samuel Element.

Edward Paget-Tomlinson's drawing depicts a wooden joey boat on the bank at Valencia Wharf undergoing repair. With the final decline of commercial carrying on the BCN in the 1960s, the Allens turned their skills to building pleasure craft for the growing boating fraternity. During this period they also changed from making boats of wood to boats of steel.

Bob and Tom Allen continued the boatyard business after the death of their father, Les. Valencia Wharf, at this time, comprised two basins. Boats were assembled on the bank placed between the two arms. Part of the site included a covered building where the early stages of construction were carried out, and some of the later stages, such as painting. All stores were kept in a wooden shed constructed from boat bottoms, which probably dated from the time Elements had the wharf. When the yard closed, this shed was demolished.

Allen's Yard was always a cluttered place where boats under repair and construction lined the banks, and a collection of other craft was moored along the canalside. Here was a place on the BCN where time almost stood still whilst all about it was changing. The buildings beside the towpath at Whimsey Bridge were demolished, the Oldbury Loop was filled in, and Whimsey Bridge itself was eventually rebuilt as part of the Churchbridge road-widening scheme. Churchbridge widening also caused the demolition of an old mission building, which had a foundation stone with the name Walter Showell (the Langley Brewery owner) inscribed as well of the names of members of the Element family stamped into the brickwork.

The mission building belonged to a different age when the area around the canal had brickworks and collieries at work, and the spiritual needs of the workers and miners were looked after by the ministers based there. Whimsey Bridge appears to take its name from Whimsey Colliery that had a number of shafts west of the canal that were linked by tramroads to basins beside the canal, one of which formed part of Valencia Wharf, in later times.

Valencia is a modern name for the wharf; the original spelling was *Valentia,* and it is this version that appears on all

Valencia Wharf 2009. The long branch canal that was the Valencia Arm was infilled to a short length near the Old Main line at Oldbury, to provide more space for Holloways' lorries. The stub of canal was retained to serve Allen's boat yard.
Brenda Ward

Les Allen's boatyard at Valencia Wharf.
Max Sinclair

nineteenth century and early twentieth century maps that show it. The canalside here had a long and changing history. When the BCN was first made through Oldbury in the years 1769 and 1770, the route followed a winding course through the centre of the town. At the spot where Valencia Wharf came to be made, the canal crossed a small stream before turning eastwards towards Oldbury. During 1820 the BCN proprietors had the Old Main Line straightened at this point driving a new line of canal from the aqueduct through to the Brades, relegating the part of the old line through Oldbury to loop status. The junction became known as Oldbury Old Turn (East End).

There were ultimately five basins opposite the junction with the Oldbury Loop. The first pair was established during the early part of the nineteenth century to serve mines that raised both coal and ironstone. The others were made later to serve various brickworks and by 1857, all five had been established. The first basin of the group (if seen from Seven Stars Bridge) was gradually extended during the 1860s and early 1870s. It passed under Park Street, and terminated near the shafts of the old Whimsey Colliery that had been renamed Valentia Colliery. Mineral statistics for the period record Whitehouse & Smith as owners of the mine.

The extended basin became known as both the Valentia Arm and Churchbridge Branch. In addition to Valentia Colliery, this branch also served Churchbridge brickworks and Highfield Colliery.

Chance & Hunt, chemical manufacturers, also established a boat dock beside the Valentia Arm, where they maintained their fleet of boats. A Belfast roofed shed covered one part of the yard, which bordered the south side of the arm near the junction with the Old Main Line. The once independent chemical manufacturing firms of Chance Brothers (Oldbury) and Hunts & Sons (Wednesbury) had combined in 1898 to form Chance & Hunt. Part of the Chance & Hunt fleet comprised craft specially adapted for the carriage of gas water or tar water from the gas works to their chemical works where it was processed. Other more conventional craft carried muriatic and sulphuring acid in carboys to canal side metal works and rolling mills, where they were used to clean ferrous and non-ferrous metals following annealing. Chance & Hunt was also an early user of motor tugs on the BCN. They had a pair of tugs called the *Hector* and *Stentor*. Walker Brothers, of Rickmansworth completed the first of the pair in 1916.

Much of the land around Valentia Wharf was later owned by ICI, who took over the chemical interests of Chance & Hunt, and then Joseph Holloway. T & S Element leased Valentia Wharf from ICI and sublet the wharf to Les Allen & Sons. Following colliery and brickyard closures, the Valentia Arm was eventually filled in throughout its entire length. It was the next two basins which became part of Allen's Boatyard and the modern *Valencia* Wharf. The first of the Allen basins had been constructed to serve the needs of Radnalfield (sometimes called Radnall Field) Brickworks and Colliery, which at one time was owned by Wood & Ivery. The mine, established first, covered some 30 acres of mineral property that had seams of Brooch, Heathen, New Mine and Thick Coal as well as Gubbin and New Mine Ironstone. The surface plant included a steam winding engine, pumping engine, and pit head gear, but little else. 600 yards of horse drawn tramway linked the pithead with the canal basin wharf, where the different grades of coal and ironstone were sorted into boats by the loaders. The brickworks was constructed after 1876 to work a layer of good quality surface clay. After the brickyard opened, the tramway was used to bring bricks down to the wharf for loading into boats.

T & S element horse drawn boat, based from Valentia Wharf.

The second of the Allen basins, and the third of the group, served the glassworks of W E Chance. Known as the Oldbury Glassworks, this works made it their speciality to produce glass lampshades. Basin No. 4 served the Churchbridge Tube Works that belonged to the firm Accles & Pollock. Accles had previously been involved with ammunition, cycle and motorcar making at the Holford Mills, Witton, but when this business failed, in 1901, had transferred to the Churchbridge Works. Accles & Pollock were later to enlarge their business through the construction of the Paddock Tube Works, on former brickyard land north of Whimsey Bridge. J & S Tonks used basin No. 5 as a coal wharf. These Birmingham based coal merchants carried coal to Paddock Tube Works from the Cannock Chase Collieries.

Hecla, built by the Allens at Valencia Wharf, is seen here passing by the remains of the wharf. The paint scheme was designed by Edward Paget-Tomlinson, with the lettering painted as 'Valentia Wharf'.

Beyond the five basins was Park Hall Wharf that served Morris's Brickworks, a Hay Wharf and finally Whimsey Bridge. The firm of T & S Element still have their road haulage depot at Whimsey Bridge. Elements, who ceased canal carrying during the 1960s, once had several canalside wharves in the Oldbury area. Their stables at Whimsey Bridge were latterly used by Caggy Stevens, but have now been demolished.

It seems that every inch of the canalside around Whimsey Bridge had some canal function. Adaptation was the theme of many BCN wharves and basins, which ensured their longevity. Thus it was that mine wharves were adapted for other purposes. Boatbuilding was the last canal related trade carried on here.

Why the name changed from Valentia to Valencia may have been the result of someone seeking to form a link with the Spanish City. This City and Region has no obvious association with Oldbury, but the original name Valentia appears to have a more logical connection with Ireland. Irish labourers frequently found employment in Black Country mines. When the mine owners christened their colliery, Valentia, it may well have been done to remember Valentia on the coast of Southern Ireland. The bleak and windswept Irish Valentia coastline has more similarity with industrial Oldbury than the sun drenched orange groves of Spanish Valencia.

Les Allen's yard at Valencia Wharf, with Staffordshire & Worcestershire Canal 1898 wooden inspection launch *Lady Hatherton* undergoing major repairs. Coincidentally, as this book is published, further major work is being completed at the boatyard at Malkins Bank on the Trent & Mersey Canal, near Sandbach.

Max Sinclair

W is for Witton

The construction of the Tame Valley Canal brought new communications to Perry Barr and Witton, which had hitherto been served by the turnpike road. This stretch of waterway was opened in 1844, and formed part of a new canal link from Salford Bridge through Perry Barr to Wednesbury, and the many varied industries located alongside the Walsall Canal. The completion, in 1847, of the Rushall Canal was to forge another link between the Tame Valley Canal and the Daw End Branch, which was to provide a direct communication with the Cannock Chase Coalfield.

A new colliery sinking at Hamstead, near Great Barr, between 1875 and 1880, brought coals directly to the Tame Valley Canal once the pit was finished. Hamstead was one of the deepest mines in the region and one of the most dangerous. Coal seams bursting into flames were a constant problem. Production was disrupted from time to time through serious fires, but the mine continued to draw coal until 1965. A second colliery established by the Perry Colliery Company found little coal and this venture was abandoned. The shafts were retained and used to draw water for Birmingham Corporation, and briefly for the BCN. In recent years British Waterways have again used the Perry Well as a supply to feed water into the Tame Valley Canal.

Witton was on the fringes of Birmingham and part of Aston Parish. Early industry had been confined to water powered mills during the eighteenth century, but with the growing industrial conurbation, developers came to covet the green fields of Witton that lined the River Tame. George Kynoch set the trend when he moved his ammunition making plant out from the centre of Birmingham during the 1870s. Other ammunition makers followed, with the acquisition of the Holford Mills. George Kynoch had been a partner in a small percussion cap manufactory known as Pursall's Hampton Street Works. Birmingham was then the heart of the cap making industry, but following a number of serious explosions, cap makers were encouraged to move the cap filling part of the process out to the countryside where subsequent accidents would not endanger people living and working close to the cap factories. Those that did the cap filling had, of course to accept the risk!

Kynoch transferred his cap factory to Witton where he set up the Lion Works. Holford Mill was a water mill that drew water from a pool north of the mill buildings. The original mill buildings appear to have been erected during the fourteenth century when Roger of Wyrley established a Fulling Mill. During its long existence, Holford Mill served successively as a hammer mill, blade mill and a rolling mill. By 1839, the tenant Thomas Clowes made gun barrels there, and this arms link was continued

The GEC works at Witton on the Tame Valley Canal, with several day boats moored up, and the telpher in the distance. *HNBC Weaver Collection*

when the mill and adjacent land were acquired for development by a new arms company that became known as the National Arms & Ammunition Co Ltd. This firm operated a number of premises in the Birmingham district. They were formed in 1872 and advertised a share issue in 1874. Both the Earl of Lichfield and Westley Richards were then listed amongst the directors. The National Arms & Ammunition Company ceased trading during the 1890s, and Holford Mills passed to the Gatling Gun Company, then Accles Ltd., before Kynochs took over the premises in 1901.

The Kynoch site was extensive, and came to cover the land between the London & North Western Railway and the Tame Valley Canal. To the south of the vast Kynoch site, the General Electric Company acquired another 110 acres. This area of land extended from the LNWR Sutton Coldfield Branch to Deykin Avenue and along both sides of the Tame Valley Canal. Prior to the GEC developments, the area was a collection of fields that ran up alongside the bottom two locks of the Perry Barr flight. Apart from the locks, there were BCN cottages and a pumping engine. The Perry Barr Engines were located in an engine house on the south side of Deykin Avenue Bridge, and were used to re-circulate water from the bottom to the top of the locks. These engines were in use between 1851 and 1958 and were the last of the BCN pumping engines to be used. Towing paths also extended along both sides of the canal at this point

The GEC commenced manufacture at Witton during 1902. They came to make a range of different electric goods and plant at Witton, and the demands of such a site eventually led to the company building an electrical generating plant there. The generation of power relied on the use of steam turbines and steady supply of coal was needed for the boilers. Canal-borne coal was delivered by narrow boat to a wharf on the Tame Valley.

A length of towpath was utilised for the wharf, and boat horses were directed to use the other path by a roving bridge. The power house was placed between the mica shop and test room. It was later enlarged to take over the mica shop site. The new powerhouse was provided with an overhead telpher that would unload coal boats by mechanical grab. It is this latter period which is depicted in Edward Paget-Tomlinson's drawing.

Coal and slack were supplied to the GEC works at Witton from various mines. Coal contractors that included T & S Element, T Foster, T Boston, Samuel Barlow, Bradbury, Son & Co, H Ilsley & Sons and Leonard Leigh, brought coal from mines that included Aldridge, Cannock & Leacroft, Conduit, Coppice, Grove, Hamstead, Holly Bank, Mid Cannock, Old Coppice and Pooley Hall. There was also a requirement for coke that came by boat from local gasworks such as Windsor Street, and creosote that also came by boat from the tar distilleries at Oldbury. Rubbish was taken away by boat to local tips.

There is little evidence to show that any of the GEC products were despatched by boat. They appear to have been sent out of the gates by road and transferred where necessary to rail. Even though the GEC works at Witton were located beside the railway, no railway sidings were ever put into the works, even though there was a link proposed during the First World War.

Hardy Spicer was another firm to establish a canal side factory in Witton. Hardy Spicer made flexible couplings for automotive transmissions. They opened a new factory at Chester Road, Erdington in 1955 and sent components from their factory above the lock at Deykin Avenue along the Birmingham & Fazeley Canal to a new wharf near Tyburn. Push tugs were used to propel open boats along the waterway at a time when canal traffic was in decline. Regrettably this service was relatively short lived and industrial problems are believed to be the cause for the cessation of this trade during the mid 1960s.

Today, the Witton canal scene has changed considerably. Most of the GEC Works and Power Plant were demolished during the 1990s, although traffic in canal-borne coal and slack ceased in the 1960s. The Perry Barr pumping house and some of the canal cottages have also now gone, and only the Deykin Avenue Lock house remains to remind canal enthusiasts of former times.

E.W. PAGET-TOMLINSON NOV 2

X is for Cross Roads

There are many features and facets to be found on the BCN. One of the most unusual is the canal crossroads where two waterways cross on the level. Canals might feed in to rivers, and river navigations are sometimes the meeting point of more than one canal. Canal crossing canal at the same level is frequently encountered where a shorter route was constructed across the course of a contour canal. Several examples are encountered on the Oxford Canal where the old route is frequently

marked, and spanned, by a Horseley Company towpath bridge.

The BCN also had its share of crossroads created through shortenings of the Old Main Line, at the Brades (Oldbury) and on the long section from Smethwick to Birmingham at Ladywood (Birmingham), Pudding Green (West Bromwich) and the Soap Works (Smethwick). The group

Rotton Park/Eyre Street Junction. The canal cross roads in Ladywood was created when the original old main line (Brindley/Simcox) was cut through to make the New Main line for Thomas Telford during the years 1826-1827. The crossroads thus created had bridges for the north and south towpaths and a bridge that united both towpaths. The segments of the old main line became the Icknield Port Loop and the Winson Green Loop. In this view, as seen from the Winson Green Loop, the 1854 North Towpath bridge is seen spanning the Icknield Port Loop. The Docker Brother paint factory is on the left and Inco Alloy Products on the right. The remains of the wharf for the Victoria Bedstead works was also on the right just beyond the 1854 side bridge.
BCNS Archive

of small loops at Oldbury was lost many years ago and the crossroads at Pudding Green Junction became a simple junction between the main line and Walsall Canal when the Izon's loop was filled in. A less obvious crossing point was the route from the Cape Arm across the main line into the Soap Works basin, which once formed part of the old main line through the Soho Foundry. The Cape Arm junction was altered during construction of the New Main Line, and the reservoir feeder and boat movement would have been either to or from the Cape Arm or the Soap Works.

Two crossroads near Birmingham remain, and see regular boat movements from any direction. Distance tables give two names to each of these junctions. The first, opposite what is now The Barclaycard Arena (originally the National Indoor Arena), was known as both Old Turn Junction and Deep Cutting Junction, whilst the second was called either Rotton Park Junction or Eyre Street Junction. Both junctions mark the crossing of Brindley's old contour canal completed in 1769 and the newer direct route as engineered by Thomas Telford and built between 1826 and 1827.

Edward Paget-Tomlinson's drawing depicts a busy scene at Rotton Park Junction. This is the only crossing on the BCN where the two canals cross almost at right angles, and for this reason is quite an unusual feature. All craft have to take special caution when passing through this point, particularly for horse boaters whose lines had either chosen to follow the route dictated by the roving bridges, or unpeg their horses and pole their craft across. The junction came into existence when the Telford route was constructed across the Ladywood Valley. The dip in land is not obvious now but there was a valley and a stream that ran down from Rotton Park. Telford arranged to dam the upper part to make the BCN Reservoir, but the drop in land remained encapsulated within the loop and then opened outwards towards the turnpike road at Spring Hill. The making of the Ladywood embankment completely enclosed the valley land between the loop of the old waterway and the new canal. With time, this piece of land was made up to the level elsewhere and used for industrial purposes and a couple of boat building yards.

The making of the Stour Valley Railway provided another barrier across the valley when it was constructed during the years 1848-1851. Land between the Canal and Railway on the stretch of railway from New Street Tunnel to Eyre Street was developed as railway coal wharves and a canal interchange basin. The London & North Western Railway, which operated the Stour Valley Railway from the opening of the line in 1852, also erected a locomotive shed and carriage shed on this stretch of railway. The railway at New Street Station is well below canal level but once through the tunnel it climbs steadily to pass over the BCN Old Main Line by a low bridge close to Rotton Park Junction. Here the railway forms a junction in its own right. The Harborne branch joined the main line here and the towpath wall is specially reinforced to take the branch railway as it climbed to cross

1976 - Caggy Stevens on his tug *Caggy* at Icknield Port, towing an assortment of boats from the direction of Birmingham. The Soho Loop (the 'old' main line) crosses the 'new' main line.   *BCNS Archives*

over the main line a few hundred yards north of Rotton Park canal junction.

Industry was crammed into every spot along the route of the old main line as it curved through Winson Green and Birmingham Heath. Both sides of the Icknield Port Loop were utilised as well as parts of the New Main Line from Old Turn through to Rotton Park Junction, and railway sidings occupied most of the rest.

The drawing is a view of the junction looking from the Icknield Port Loop across the Main Line towards Birmingham Heath, and depicts a view about 1920 when a London & Western tank engine is shown to be heading towards the bridge. The Old Main Line was lined then, as now, with factories and works on both sides. The view through the bridge on the right hand side was to see an almost continuous line of brickwork that extended round the corner to Springhill Bridge, and included the rolling mills of Earl Bourne & Co and Barker & Allen. On the left of this view is the towpath and the side bridge that spanned the entrance to Springhill Basin.

Springhill Basin was made about 1838 and was originally a long basin that ran the length of Eyre Street. In fact it was sometimes referred to as Eyre Street Basin as it runs the complete length of this street. Early wharf accommodation was let to a coal merchant, Samuel Thornley, varnish maker, of Lionel Street and J.Singleton, Manufacturing Chemist. Thornley established a colour manufactory with William Badhams to make colours for paint manufacturers. Other parts of the Thornley estate were developed during the 1860s as a sheet ironworks and a tube rolling mill. Another plot adjacent to Springhill Basin was acquired by Hadley Brothers to make cut nails. The nail works increased in size and operation and finally took over the colour and rolling mills sites.

On the other side of Rotton Park Junction, one corner of the canal was occupied by PPG, whose customers include the car industry. They had a long frontage along the Old Main line that extends down to Icknield Port Bridge. Their business has taken over several other adjacent works to reach its present size and include much of the former McKechnie Brothers non-ferrous metal works. The PPG paint manufactory, in Rotton Park Street, began as varnish factory established by Docker Brothers, who specialised in supplying varnish for coachwork and railway rolling stock. Their business after several takeovers became part of the modern PPG group. Another part of their works occupied the former Lovekin's boatyard site. Narrow gauge track still remains buried in the towpath facing the New Main Line. It is complete with turntable.

All the PPG works have been demolished in preparation for a new development there. The track of the tramway remains embedded in the towpath. Docker Brother records are incomplete regarding the purpose of this tramway, although it is believed that it was used to convey ash from the new boiler house for disposal by canal boat. The tramway appears to have been put down in the 1920s.

On the other side of the Old Main Line facing the PPG factory, fronting Wiggins Street, were several factories. Their number included a nickel rolling mills, weldless tube works and an early white lead works.

There is now much dereliction in this are at present although the newly improved towpath is used to the benefit of cyclists. What building walls remain, are covered in graffiti. It is truly a dismal scene.

The only remaining heritage features are the two attractive iron bridges, which span waterways on two sides. The third that carries the towpath adjacent to the railway is much more basic. In fact this bridge is a modern structure. It is likely that another bridge, possibly of Horseley make and like those at Old Turn Junction, was originally placed here when the junction was made in either 1827 or 1828. Once work had commenced on the Stour Valley Railway, the crossing of the Old Main Line may have necessitated the removal the existing bridge. Another more plausible reason has been recently suggested that bridge was damaged during the Second World War, by bombing and required replacement.

Y is for York's Bridge

The Wyrley & Essington Canal has many facets and surprises in store for those who chose to walk alongside it, or navigate its waters. Since the cessation of coal traffic, it has become a quiet BCN backwater and perhaps less used than it could be. Many opportunities exist for the boater, canoeist, cyclist or walker.

York's Bridge is located at Pelsall and has the date 1866 on the keystone. It carries Norton Road (B4154) over the canal. In the drawing, a loaded coal boat is shown to be passing under the bridge, heading in the direction of Brownhills. Behind York's Bridge is the Royal Oak Public House, which remains a canalside feature today. On the right of this picture, a moored boat is tied up alongside the edge of Pelsall Common Wharf. Many other features have been lost with the removal and relocation of industry. Most notable was the Pelsall Ironworks that lined the canal between Pelsall Works Bridge and the junction with the Cannock Extension Canal.

The origins of Pelsall Ironworks can be traced back to the years 1831 and 1832 when the Wolverhampton banker and MP, Richard Fryer, established a blast furnace and a forge on Pelsall Common adjacent to an existing coal mine on Pelsall Wood. Davis and Bloomer enlarged the Pelsall Ironworks during the 1850s and 1860s, and three separate ironworks were established alongside the waterway. The blast furnaces were also rebuilt and modernised. Coal mined at the company pits provided most of the ironworks' need for fuel, and the surplus was sold on for industrial or domestic use. The Bloomer family was instrumental in forming the Pelsall Coal & Iron Company that took over the management of the ironworks in 1873. The Pelsall Ironworks were closed in 1892 and subsequently demolished, and the last of their mines ceased work in 1903. From about 1905 until 1920, slag was broken at a cracker by the firm of John Freakley and Sons, and despatched by canal or railway for road making purposes.

Coal was mined in the neighbourhood of Pelsall long before the Wyrley & Essington Canal was made. Records exist for a Newcomen type steam engine being delivered to Pelsall Coal Works in 1717. These coal works that existed on the Common and Wood were in intermittent operation for much of the eighteenth century. Mines near the Common were re-opened during the early 1800s by James Rounds, and were subsequently worked by William James. It was during James' tenancy (c1811) that the Gilpin's Arm was cut across the Common to join the Wyrley & Essington Canal near York's Foundry Bridge.

York's Bridge with 'The Royal Oak' public house (now 'The Finger Post').

Colliery developments on Cannock Chase led to the building of the Cannock Extension Canal, which was completed as far as Hednesford Basin in 1863. Although the BCN envisaged plans for an extension as far as Rugeley, Hednesford remained the terminus. Several collieries sent coal by water along the Cannock Chase Extension to Pelsall Junction; from there it either passed through to Wolverhampton or to Brownhills, Catshill Junction and along the Rushall and Tame Valley Canals. Horse worked boats were the mainstay of the traffic until 1918, when tugs began to be used.

William G Farmer, writing in 1977, produced a detailed account of Pelsall during the early years of the twentieth century. His description of the canal trade is worth reproduction:

As one stood on Wood Common the canals were a scene of great activity. In seemingly endless procession the boats came from the various collieries with scarcely a boat's length between them. When one considers the same number of empty boats was going the other way, one gets the idea of the immensity of the traffic. The heavily laden boats, coming from the direction of Norton Canes, showed only a few inches of side above the surface of the canal, and looked about to sink. The empty ones rode high, perhaps four or more feet out of the water, and there had to be a rule of the road or should it be water, to be used in passing as the towpath is on one side only. Each boat had two men, who took it in turns to be driver or steersman. The horse pulled on a long line attached to a "mast" on the following boat, the driver urging horse on by shouts or a stick. It was amazing, the ease with which the driver flicked his rope over the mast and head of the steersman of the boat he was passing. When one looks at the grooves, inches deep, cut into the brickwork of the bridges by the ropes, one realises the millions of tons of coal transported along the canals. The public houses by the canals did a roaring trade in those days. The boatmen would tie up their boats, stable their horses, and adjourn to the pub for rest and refreshment. At holiday times when the canal was quiet, trips were organised for pleasure. Often parties would go in a cleaned out boat, or several boats, from Wilner's Bridge to Hednesford, where we had a day on the hills. Probably, people nowadays would not think much of such an outing, but we found it enjoyable. As the numbers of heavy road lorries increased, so traffic on the canals declined, accelerated by the closing of many local mines. Some users had tugs pulling a number of barges at a time, but this seems to have been ended now, at any rate in this district.

The biggest threat to traffic was ice in winter. Pelsall Common was, and is, a vast open space, with little shelter from the rain, wind or snow and the wind-chill factor was greater here than other parts of the BCN network. Icebreakers were usually stationed on this part of the BCN network to ensure that the boats kept moving.

William Farmer had the following recollections about the icebreakers:

In the winter the canals were kept usable by the means of the icebreaker. This was a fairly short boat, with a heavy iron keel, made especially for the job. It had a wooden platform on top, with a heavy rail down the middle running the length of the boat. Men stood on each side of the rail and as the boat started to move, they rocked the boat from side to side. Pulled by a large team of horses, the heavy keel, helped by the rocking, soon made a way through the ice. What with the shouting, and loud cracking and crunching of the ice, it was very interesting and there was always a crowd of onlookers. There were two of these icebreakers, pulled out of the water in summer, and stationed at the stop on the Wood Common.

Periodically, severe frosts might occur and there were times, in some years, when the canal was blocked with ice for weeks at a time and supplies to Birmingham and Black Country industry were stopped. William Farmer recalled a time during one particularly bad winter when serious disruption occurred to trade:

In the First World War there was an eleven-week frost, the canals became frozen and the coal barges became ice-bound. The position was serious, as the canals were the chief means of conveying coal, the lifeblood of industry to users in munitions works and power plants in the midlands. The few petrol lorries, and indeed even horses, were commandeered by the army. When the icebreakers finally got through, the lumps of ice jammed together and the boats again were stuck. Mr Arthur Wilkes, son of Ernest Wilkes, the owner of the foundry, made a kind of conveyor, worked by a petrol engine. This was taken to Fishley, where the canal had a steep embankment, and installed there. Troops were brought in and pushed the masses of ice towards the conveyor. The ice rode out of the canal on an endless belt and crashed down the bank. After a few days the boats were free to move again, and the device was stopped working because the loss of ice was lowering the level of water in the canal.

The last time the trade on the BCN was stopped by ice happened during the winter of 1962 and 1963, at the time when the British Waterway Board replaced the British Transport Commission. The ice was so bad on this occasion that the icebreakers broke the ice so often that no water was left to maintain traffic.

William Farmer's recollections mention the 'Wilkes' Foundry. This was known as the Pelsall Foundry, which was located near the Church. Pelsall Foundry made a range of steam driven plant for local industry and was one of three local foundries that supplied plant for coal mines, limestone workings, brickyards and ironworks. The other two were known as the Goscote Foundry and York's Foundry.

Goscote Foundry was the oldest of the three, having been established about 1800, and included amongst its services the boring of cylinders for early steam engines. This foundry was located beside the road that led to Goscote Works Bridge. York's Foundry was a small foundry, which bounded the towpath on the east side of York's Foundry Bridge. Trade directories for the 1860s list the proprietors as Messrs York, Ball & Fearon.

York's Foundry and Goscote Foundry have long gone, but their names live on with the naming of the bridges. Pelsall Foundry records survive and are kept at the Walsall Archives Centre and provide an invaluable source of information about this company. Other reminders of the past are the surviving canal features that include Pelsall Works Bridge (metalwork supplied by the Horseley Iron Company in 1824), the Red Iron Bridge (at Pelsall Junction) and the group of old canal cottages (211 & 212) plus a stable block at Friars Bridge.

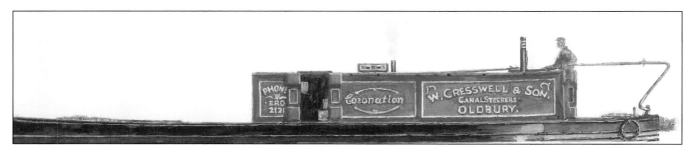

W Cresswell & Son's tug *Coronation*.

Z is for Zinc

Zinc is a metal which has several important uses. It forms an important constituent of the various brass alloys, for which the town of Birmingham gained a world-wide reputation. Brass is an alloy of copper and zinc, where the proportion of copper and zinc was varied to produce brass for specific purposes. Copper was present in the largest amount and often comprised up to two-thirds of the alloy. The Zinc content rose to a third, but other metals such as tin and lead might also be present in small amounts.

The marriage of copper and zinc to make brass was initially achieved through the heating of copper and a zinc ore known as calamine. It was a process that used up large quantities of coal that was required to heat the melting pots. Birmingham's brass working industry preceded the making of brass in the area, but the price of brass purchased from existing brass making districts, such as Bristol, or Cheadle in Staffordshire, fluctuated at the whim of the brass manufacturers. Birmingham businessmen believed that they could make cheaper brass themselves.

The Birmingham Metal Company, established in 1780, was a syndicate of local businessmen whose aim was to buy brass and pass on the corporate benefits of group buying to their members. They decided to make brass in Birmingham and purchased land for a brassworks. The site chosen was located alongside the turnpike road, then known as Islington and formed a triangular plot of land that was bordered on one side by the line of the Birmingham Canal. Land levels varied at this point. The canal, at this point, was constructed through the hillside in what was called the Deep Cutting. It passed under the Turnpike Road and then curved round to reach the Old Wharf that faced Paradise Street. The Brassworks offices faced Islington (later Broad Street), whilst the works were located, to the rear, on land that dipped down to the level of the canal, where a wharf was made.

Neither calamine nor copper was available locally. Calamine was brought from Derbyshire, whilst an important supply of copper metal was the Swansea district of South Wales, where there were a number of different copper works. Birmingham brass founders and brass workers were associated with two copper works, Birmingham and Rose, located north of Swansea beside the River Tawe. Copper (in tile, strip or ingot form) was transported by coastal vessels, then Severn River trows (or barges), and finally canal boats to reach Birmingham. Brassworkers and brass founders who held shares in either the Rose

1970 - Deep Cutting from the site of the church that spanned the canal here. The former brassworks building is on the left, and the former brewery buildings on the right. Old Turn Junction bridge is in the distance; beyond it is now the Barclaycard Arena. The whole area has been extensively redeveloped, and is now known as Brindleyplace. *Bob May*

Copper Company or the Birmingham Mining and Copper had a small allotment of copper, and paid a specific rate for the different types copper. Other Swansea based copper companies also had offices in Birmingham, such was the demand for copper. Ingot brass might also be supplied.

The Birmingham Brassworks was one of four located in the West Midlands. Of the other three brassworks, two were located beside the Birmingham Canal at Smethwick and Spon Lane, whilst the third was placed alongside the Trent & Mersey Canal at Stone. Canals were integral to the transport of coal, copper and calamine.

A sales advert for Smethwick Brassworks, published in March 1789, described this works as equipped with apparatus and utensils of every kind used in the making of ingot brass and trading under the name of Thomas Salt and the Old Birmingham Brass Company. The brassworks were then capable of making about 200 tons of brass a year. A horse mill was used to grind the calamine that went into the pots. A plot of land was leased near Matlock, Derbyshire where calamine was brought for dressing, and the brass ingots were taken in Birmingham to a warehouse in Edmund Street.

Smethwick Brassworks were erected beside the Smethwick Locks when the flight comprised six separate locks. Wharf space was available between the fourth and fifth lock on the flight. The top three locks were removed between 1789 and 1790 when the Summit was lowered to the 473 ft (o.d.) level. The canal changes led to the Brasshouse wharf being altered to give access to the lower level.

Edward Paget-Tomlinson's last drawing depicts the Brasshouse in Birmingham and is a fine interpretation of the engraving published in Bisset's directory. It shows the towpath and wharf, three brass cones, brassworks and offices. The canal towpath was opposite the Brassworks. The second towpath that runs alongside the Brassworks was added about the time of Telford's improvements to the BCN. The exact date when this section of towpath was made remains to be established.

The calamine method fell out of favour as metallic Zinc became more readily available. All West Midlands brassworks closed during the 1830s when spelter (zinc metal) came to be brought into the region by boat. The Birmingham Brassworks was advertised for sale in June 1830, when the premises comprised committee rooms, offices, workmen's houses, packing, stores and metal rooms, with six melting houses, capable of making ten tons of brass per week.

Thomas Pemberton became proprietor of the Birmingham Brasshouse in 1831. The buildings were principally used as a metal warehouse although some brass continued to be made there until about 1850. The brass appears to have been made through the improved method of mixing spelter and copper. Rate books for this later period show that Pemberton owned an extensive property, which included warehouses, shops, a steam engine and machinery.

Although the old Brassworks buildings were pulled down a long time ago, the offices and committee rooms have survived and still front Broad Street. They are now like many Broad Street premises converted for the leisure trade and are licensed for the sale of alcohol, but the Georgian frontage is excellently preserved.

Smethwick Brassworks were advertised again for sale in 1834. The works then comprised three smelting houses with furnaces, a horse mill, pothouse, stabling, warehouse, counting house and a dwelling house. Brass making at Smethwick ceased about this time and the premises converted into other uses. William Beasley and William Farmer made gun barrels there and by 1867 the premises had become the property of the District Iron & Steel Company.

Brass founders started to mix spelter and copper to form the brass, and produce castings needed for different purposes. Another basic use of brass metal was as strip, which was rolled from ingot brass by rolled metal manufacturers. Brass strip went from the rolling mill to the pressworker or die stamper to be made into a final product. A third use was brass wire, which was made by drawing ingots through dies until a specified diameter was achieved. Birmingham, noted for its diversity in trades, utilised all these skills to best advantage. Emerging industries included bedsteads, cabinet brass foundry, gas fittings, nail, pin and screw makers.

Transport of both copper and spelter was through the offices of the merchandise canal carrier and also the railway companies, once the rail network was established during the 1850s. Canal side warehouses and wharves provided an important link in the supply chain and certain carriers' depots were the focus of the spelter and copper trade.

Another use of zinc was as a protective coating for iron and steel. The process, known as galvanising, was developed during the 1840s and led to the establishment of a number of galvanising plants in Birmingham and the Black Country. Many were canal based and received spelter, iron and coal by boat. The process of galvanising consisted of:

Cleaning the surface of the article, with acid
Coating the surface with a flux
Finally immersing the article in a bath of molten zinc.

Galvanising works required coal to heat the zinc dipping baths and acid from local chemical works to clean and pickle the iron. Manufacturers, however, found that gas fired baths proved more suitable for their trade.

Canal carriage of spelter continued well into the twentieth century. Traffic returns as late as 1928 reveal Ash & Lacy Ltd, Globe Galvanising Works, Great Bridge and Stewarts and Lloyds, Coombeswood Tubeworks, received spelter from London in Fellows, Morton & Clayton Boats. Bantocks also carried spelter from Hawne Basin railway interchange basin to Coombeswood.

Fellows, Morton & Clayton, and their successors British Waterways, continued to carry copper and spelter by canal into the Birmingham wharves. Robert Wilson refers to the British Waterways spelter trade in his book 'Too Many Boats'. Back loads from London included copper cathodes and billets, spelter, aluminium ingots and steel. It was a traffic that declined, and finally ceased, after 1960.

There is still a requirement for zinc in the making of brass strip, wire and ingots as well as in the galvanising trade. Birmingham still has its share of rolled metal manufacturers, brass founders and galvanisers, and still receives supplies of copper and zinc metal as new cast ingots or recycled scrap. The only difference is that nothing is brought by canal, or rail. Road transport is now the means of transporting both raw ingredients and final products.

Stewarts & Lloyds tug no. 4, based at Coombeswood Tube Works.

Phillips & Son's bedstead factory, Speedwell Works, on Sherborne Street. Several similar factories were built canalside, as raw materials arrived that way, and presumably finished would have left by canal. Phillips had an arm off the Oozells Branch. The factory used strip casting to mix zinc and copper to make brass.

INDEX

Also published or distributed by Canal Book Shop - www.canalbookshop.co.uk

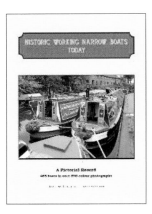

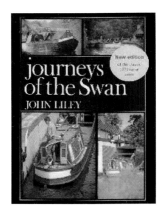

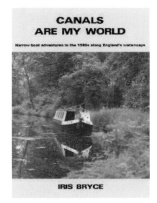

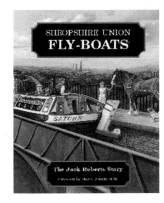